SKYROCKET TEAMS

To

INCREDIBLE HEIGHTS

Motivate and Empower,
Improve Group Performance,
Sustain Excellent Team Dynamics,
Collaborate & Achieve Exceptional Goals.

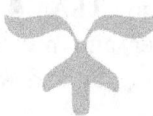

GITA RAMACHANDRAN

https://gitaramachandran.com/

DEDICATION

I dedicate this book to:

My parents, Late **Lt. Col. N. Chandrasekharan**, and Late Mrs. **Padmavathy Chandrasekharan**, who inspired me to dream, decide and do what I desired.

My companion **Mr. K.V. Ramachandran** who stood by me, and helped me in completing this creative piece.

My children **Kavita Ramachandran** and **Kiran Ramachandran**, who have been my critiques as well as pillars of strength in improving my credentials in my authorship journey.

My Children in-law **Ranjith Nambiar** and **Anju Govind**, who have provided valuable tips and helped me in editing my manuscript.

My **Siblings**, **Extended Family**, and **Friends**, who have always stood by me and supported me.

My love to my grandchildren **Rohini, Aathira, Anikaa,** and **Aadya.**

Last but not the least, my **TEAMS** at different phases of my corporate career and my life, who were the **INCREDIBLES** all the way and whom I consider as my own family

Gita Ramachandran
https://gitaramachandran.com/

SKYROCKET TEAMS	0
To	0
INCREDIBLE HEIGHTS	0
DEDICATION	1
INTRODUCTION	4
Chapter 1	12
COMMON PURPOSE	12
Chapter 2	21
EFFECTIVE LEADERSHIP	21
Chapter 3	36
ROLES, RESPONSIBILITIES, RELATIONSHIPS	36
Roles	37
Responsibilities	42
Relationships	45
Chapter 4	52
TEAM EFFECTIVENESS	52
Characteristics	53
Principles	55
Strategies	59
Dysfunctional Teams	61
Chapter 5	68
HOW TO BE INCREDIBLES	68
Key Areas for Effectiveness	68
Effective Procedures / Processes	72
The Journey to Incredible Performance	83
Monitoring and maintaining consistency	86
Chapter 6	94
CONFLICT RESOLUTION	94
About conflict:	94
Conflicts within the team and how to handle them:	98
Approaches to deal with conflict	100
Chapter 7	107
COMMUNICATION	107
Chapter 8	117
CONCLUSION	117

May I ask you for a small favor? 125
Other Books in Scaling up the Corporate Ladder Series 126
BIBLIOGRAPHY 127
ACKNOWLEDGEMENTS...................................128
COPYRIGHT 128

INTRODUCTION

"Individual commitment to a group effort—that makes a team work, a company work, a society work, a civilization work." --Vince Lombardi

Have you not noticed that many a time, teams with ordinary performers, achieve far more than the team with outstanding individuals? Have you wondered why this is happening, when all would have bet on the team with outstanding performers to have won the game? It may be worthwhile to note that what distinguishes between the success and failure of any project is a great team. One may have umpteen individual star performers in one's team, but if they are not operating based on the principles of team effectiveness, then that team is not going to deliver excellent results.

Despite having the best individual performers, if one's team is struggling to level up, then one needs to sit back, analyze why it is so, and take corrective actions.

Let us first delve into the research done by an eminent personality Dr. Raymond Meredith Belbin on team roles. He is a leading authority who researched for over 40 years and came up with the theory of how more important it is for team members to fit together, than on how smart they individually were.

Experts can determine if an individual will become a business superstar or not using the personality tests as developed by Dr Belbin's research. Those who passed with flying colors were cleverer, had better analytical and logical skills, and were better than others in almost every aspect.

A skilled team was formed comprising of these outstanding individuals for research and was named the Apollo team. Everyone thought that the superstars of the Apollo team would achieve success. However, contrary to expectations, the team made of the strongest individuals performed worse than a regular team. The Apollo team members spent most of their time debating and trying to convince other members that their point of view was the correct one. No one was ready to change their point of view. Each one tried to find loopholes in each other's arguments and stuck to their stand. The team couldn't reach any decision and all pressing jobs were neglected.

This happens when you put only superstars together and expect them to deliver exceptional results. It is very difficult to make all team members put aside their egos, trust one another, and act as a responsible team. If we can respect and trust one another despite our disagreements, then only we will be able to see the value the other member brings to the table. Abandoning ego and cooperating allows one to become part of a whole, that is greater than the sum of its parts.

The only way to build a successful organization is to build elite teams which will deliver stellar performance. To enable this, the teams should have team leaders who are effective and passionate about building talented and effective teams. No matter how smart, talented, driven, or passionate one is, his success as a team leader will depend on his ability to build and inspire his/her team. A successful leader can motivate his or her team members to work together towards a common vision, a common purpose, or a goal.

However, if despite all the best efforts by the team leader, if even one team member slackens, or takes the task casually, or does not deliver, his effort at building a great team would fail and he would not achieve results as envisaged. We are as strong as the weakest link only. Team leaders will have to communicate, inspire and motivate their team members, to align and attune them to the common objective.

In addition to an effective communication process, the leader will need to focus on other aspects which can make his team incredible, inspired, and ingenious to deliver and raring to go. Finding out what makes a team click and what makes it dysfunctional, as well as taking necessary corrective actions, and putting the right processes and framework in place, will go a long way in making one's team effective, incredible, and ready to deliver exceptional value and extraordinary results.

We cannot rule out conflicts arising in a team comprising of diverse team members of differing caliber. Conflicts need to be evened out. For that, the teams will have to put a proper mechanism in place for resolving conflicts, which will vary on case to case basis.

What are the changes required to be incorporated to remove clashes, ego tussles, and conflicts? How can we get each team member to be hungry to achieve, be helpful to one another and collaborate, be passionate and persistent to deliver results, as well as command respect? Read this book to get your answers.

For any organization to be successful, its projects should be successful and deliver expected or more than expected results. For this to happen, there should be high-performing teams, led by effective team leaders. As teams are bound to either just perform or underperform if not taken care of from the beginning, one needs to take steps to communicate and motivate large, diverse groups to tackle complex projects. With effective communication as well countless other things described in this book, including the process framework and conflict resolution mechanism, one can increase the groups' emotional intelligence, make the team perform well, and elevate it to an *incredible, invincible, and inexorable team.*

Let's understand and break down the components of success and start from the basics by considering the most important deliverables of teamwork- **the outcome.**

Final Outcome
We form a team to meet the clear goals of accomplishing certain result or aim, that as an individual, one cannot achieve alone. Those results need to be measurable to decide the effectiveness of the team performance, and it has to function based on a few criteria described below, which have emerged from the discussions above.

The essentials for the functioning of a high-performance team are as under:

Sl no	Icon	Components description
1		The team has <u>a ***common purpose***</u> or a goal or a mission to be accomplished with shared values.
2		It has ***effective leadership*** in place which ensures that the team is cohesive and delivers outstanding results.

3		It has absolute clarity about the **_roles_ and _responsibilities_** to be carried out. The members are empowered to use proper resources and maintain mutually accountable and strong **_relationships._**
4		They follow certain principles and strategies and bear typical characteristics, which makes them **_effective_** and _high performers,_ and do not fall dysfunctional.
5		Their approach and method to achieve **incredible results** are aligned to a methodical process being followed with shared values.
6		They focus on resolving **_conflicts_**, conflict resolution being an important ingredient to be considered when working together in teams.
7		The _collaboration_ and **_communication_** within the team are of impeccable order.

If one wants to build a superior team that will deliver high-performance results and **_skyrocket to incredible heights_**, the best practices and ideas illustrated in this book will be of enormous help.

If one wants to reverse the fortunes of a struggling team and prevent decision deadlock, it will be worthwhile to examine and help the team overcome its particular dysfunctions by referring to the tips, guidelines, and the process stated in this book.

If you are a leader who wants to learn about an approach to increase the performance of your team, this book will be of immense value to you.

If you are an individual who wants to deliver stellar performances by being a part of a great team, then do have no doubt that you'll find the insights mentioned over here helpful, to make you achieve more than any individual can ever imagine or aspire to do so alone.

Rest assured that your team can beat the odds by boosting team performance through trust, collaboration, mutual accountability, shared values, and many nuggets explained herein.

Mr. William Burke is bang on target when he says:

"Team building is a set of activities whereby members of a work team 1) understand more thoroughly the nature of group dynamics and effective teamwork, the interrelationship of process and content or task and, 2) learn to apply certain principles and skills of group process toward greater team effectiveness."

So let us move on and study each of the points mentioned above in detail in the following Chapters as we go along and get on to Chapter 1 on **Common Purpose** and shared goals followed by other chapters as mentioned below:

- Common Purpose
- Effective Leadership
- Team members Roles Responsibilities and Relationship
- Team Effectiveness
- How to become Incredibles
- Conflict Resolution
- Communication

Chapter 1

COMMON PURPOSE

"The best teamwork comes from men who are working independently toward one goal in unison." – James Cash Penney

Definition of Team:
A team is a group of people, with complementary skills, organized to interact and work together. They are committed to a *shared common purpose, objectives, performance goals or mission*, and an approach for which they are mutually accountable. They work interdependently and share responsibility by coordinating the activities amongst themselves while holding themselves accountable individually and collectively for attaining the results.

Definition of teamwork:
Teamwork is work done by the numerous team members with each one doing a small part of the big whole, but all subordinating their self-interests to the productivity of the whole group. It helps to create a sense of belonging and a feeling of loyalty to the whole mission. Members feel more responsible for their actions and so make everything possible. So teamwork is the ability to

work as a group towards a common goal. *Teamwork thus divides the task and doubles the success.*

Teamwork depends not only on your skills but also on your attitudes as well. If you have to work together, you need to be aware of and apply interpersonal skills. Even if teams are subjected to a complicated set of challenges, it's the essentials that set the tone for successful teamwork. The secrets to successful teamwork are common purpose, shared mindset, trust, mutual accountability, collaboration, hard work, appreciation, agility, creativity, respect for one another, more of us than me, proper communication, win-win conflict resolution, and good relationship with one and all.

One can say that *teamwork, simply stated, means less of Me and more of We.*

The Common Purpose, Goal or Mission with shared values

GOALS:
For a team's purpose to be powerful, it needs to be compelling to all its members. So we need to inspire our team and make them see how each team member's work will result in an exciting, meaningful outcome, that everyone will find personally worthwhile and would want to achieve.

The common goal of any team, as it is for an individual, should be SMART, i.e. Specific, Measurable, Achievable, Relevant, and Timely. This represents the foundation for any high-performance team. The efforts of all team members are to be aligned in the same direction to meet the common objective or common purpose, which forms the main reason for their coming together as well as the basis for cooperation amongst them as members of the team.

They have to demonstrate a total commitment to the work and achievement of the common goal, which may either be short-term or long-term goals, as well as both.

Each member must understand and support the meaning and value of the team's mission and vision. Clarifying the purpose and binding it to each person's role and responsibilities augments the potential of the team. The inclusion of "stretch" goals increases the challenge necessary to motivate the team members.

Common Purpose and Shared Values:
There seems to be a shared understanding of what makes an effective group work, as no two teams are identical and there is no simple measure to assess the performance effectiveness of teams. We can say that high-performance teams are generally characterized by a combination of

purpose and goals, talents, skills, performance ethics, incentives and motivation, efficacy, leadership, conflict resolution, communication, power and empowerment, and norms and standards.

As we are on this topic of the team being bound by a common purpose, let us evaluate and find out if our team is driven by a compelling vision, strong sense of purpose, and a common set of values. Let me cite a real-life example from my professional life and decide if the team was effective in following a common purpose

Case Study:

It was in the year 1991. One day, probably in the month of Oct-Nov, I was called by my Department head who asked me to attend a particular meeting on his behalf, as he was busy. However, I was not aware of the reason and the agenda and so was not prepared. I entered the room and came face to face with the heads of various departments (HODs) including those of various Plants, Industrial Relations, Payrolls, Accounts, and groups of Employee Union leaders. I was not prepared for the barrage of words by the Union leaders who were quite upset about the arrears of salary received by the employees. A Long Term Settlement (LTS) was signed with the Union for revising their salary with effect from Jan 1976 for a period of 15 years, i.e., up to 1991. It was alleged that a lot of errors had crept in the arrears worked out and paid to the employees. No one was able to pinpoint the root cause and the HODs were clueless as to what had gone wrong, as the anomalies did not show a pattern. I was new to the department and had no inkling as to what had gone wrong but I got a gut feeling that the arrears might have to be reprocessed. After the meeting, I apprised my department head accordingly and he asked me to coordinate the activities from our department. Within a few days from the said meeting, we got a Note from the IR department asking to reprocess the arrears for the past 15 years. This was to be done based on the new terms of LTS, after fixing the fitment in the new scale for all the employees, and the payable portions to be worked out after setting off the payments already made, reckoning the relevant taxes due.

It was a tall order, as the programs were running on the mainframe DG Machine and the magnetic tapes for the 180 months had to be loaded one by one on the DG machine for this repeated exercise. The programs were written in Cobol and they were required to be corrected to reflect the new terms and conditions, applicable for each month of that year. Data was to be verified, sample reports to be taken, checked, vetted, corrected, and redone one by one, including replacement of routines for specific month correction if any.

The whole exercise was quite challenging and could again lead to possible erroneous calculations due to any inadvertent human mistakes for any specific employee, or any specific month under consideration. I had a small meeting with my team members and we together decided to simultaneously re-create the programs and data in Clipper and dBase respectively which were, compatible to be run on Personal Computers, which had started coming out in the market by then.

Our department had been set up in the late '80s and the Cobol programs for the first 10 years had been run at the head office on Mainframe computers. All programs had to be studied in detail for various rules and conditions as applicable for the payroll of each month and rewritten and compiled in Clipper, and the data was also to be recreated. The tapes for each month were loaded and processed along with Payroll inputs for that month with revised terms and conditions. The reports were verified by the Accounts Department, corrective data inputs were provided by the IR and the accuracy of the routines and results were checked and vetted by the Accounts dept. We kept running the programs written by us simultaneously in Clipper and kept them also corrected and ready in all respects along with the past and corrected inputs, systematically documented with proper naming conventions. As and when new parameters were introduced, based on testing the result of the monthly payroll, we introduced the same in the routines in Clipper too. Being compatible with

PCs, it became easier for us to correct this in the database as we could easily incorporate corrections, read and process it innumerable times, as well as for many months at one go, unlike the Cobol programs run on DG machines where the tapes had to be inserted and rerun after changing the programs for each month separately.

What was important to note here was that all of us, the team members from my team, the Accounts department, and the IR department had a common goal and common purpose ahead of us to drive us. All of us were very clear, determined, and committed to the goal of providing accurate data and results with no mistakes, whatsoever within the time frame stipulated for the same. As the goal, purpose, and mission converged, we got a complete commitment of all team members working to fulfill the same without looking at the clock. With all departments working synchronously with a focus on accurate and timely payment of arrears, it was no wonder that we broke the previous records to make error-free arrears long before the deadlines. We were aware that some data could still be challenged by a few employees. So we had kept a Plan B ready as a backup program, where the arrears could be run for one or many employees, for one month, or for many years which could be run remotely on the Novel Netware LAN. With this, the data of any employee for any month could be corrected and on reprocessing, it gave the new result after effecting the deductions for the already paid amount. On approval from the role holders concerned, any reprocessing could be carried out without the involvement of the computer department, with relevant modules to store historical data and logging the details. This meant that revised arrears could be processed for a single employee, any number of times, and data and the results would be available online with the history. This was something that was not thought of in those early days of the 1990s where data was mainly being processed on Mainframe computers. It was a great achievement for all the teams involved and it made all the stakeholders happy and satisfied with the result. This project became a WIN-WIN for all of us involved in it and others who were beneficiaries of this project.

This teamwork improved the working environment, reduced errors, kept the communication consistent and to the point, relieving stress, as all communication lines were open and transparent, and the extraordinary result was there for all to see. Compiling the wage arrears for 15 years accurately with no errors, and well before time, with a methodology to revise it for any or many employees was a singular achievement of the team.

As Henry Ford said: "Coming together is a beginning. Keeping together is progress. Working together is a success."

The best teams are those, who combine individual drive with understanding the importance of the purpose of the team, and the power of working towards common goals. This is the secret to becoming an excellent team. There is no substitute for the ongoing commitment and deliberate practice required to build better teams by chasing common goals aligned to the organizational goals.

"No matter how brilliant your mind or strategy, if you're playing a solo game, you'll always lose out to a team," says Reid Hoffman. How true!

Let's now proceed to consider the next important element of teamwork**, effective leadership**, in the next chapter as leadership plays a major part in aligning the goals of team members to that of the organization.

Chapter 2

EFFECTIVE LEADERSHIP

"You need to be aware of what others are doing, applaud their efforts, acknowledge their successes, and encourage them in their pursuits. When we all help one another, everybody wins." – Jim Stovall

Effective Leadership:
Leadership is always vital and team leadership is no exception. Leaders of high-performing teams ensure that the team remains cohesive and delivers exceptional results as per the decided timelines. Effective team leaders are flexible, service-oriented, and task-driven. They keep the purpose of the team at all times in their mind and remember that the leadership role is vested on them to serve, and not to be served. They adjust to various situations quickly and get cooperation from all at all times.

Qualities of an Effective Team leader:
A leader should be strong, decisive, empathetic, knowledgeable, supportive, and encouraging to take his/her team to new heights. He should have two main concerns, viz., the *concern for people and the concern for production*. High concern for

people will motivate the team to become more productive and high concern for production will create a sense of achievement and satisfaction for the people under him.

Expectations from a successful, trusted, and well-respected team leader:

- Effective team leaders should focus on *purpose and goals*, and make their team aware of them. They should stipulate the purpose for which the team exits in addition to keeping the purpose, goals, and approach relevant and meaningful.
- They should establish *shared ownership* for the tasks, and encourage team members to stand up and lead.
- They should *mentor and develop* team members to the fullest potential, and strive to build a stellar team and not a team of individual stars.
- They should ensure that team members constantly *enhance their skills* and provide opportunities for others, without seeking credit for themselves.
- They should *motivate and inspire* team members so that the latter build commitment and confidence in themselves.
- They should open the *lines of communication* by adopting an open-door policy at all times and resolve minor issues forthwith. They should constantly communicate with their

teams, lead, and facilitate constructive communication.
- They should *take ownership* and monitor, but avoid control and micromanaging.
- Effective team leaders should focus on relationships and manage relationships from the outside while giving a thrust on the removal of obstacles that might hinder group performance.
- They should *get their hands dirty* and do the real work required, thereby setting an example, with a firm commitment to results that will benefit the organization and each individual.

Case Study:
Let me give an example of how restructuring and reallocation of some jobs in the department helped me in motivating and inspiring my team to take up more challenging and worthwhile assignments. This also facilitated the development of all team members, who could add more and more value to the job itself.

During the erstwhile days, we had exclusive teams for the job in Electronic Data Processing (EDP) departments, segregated as Operations, Maintenance, and Projects. Everybody wanted to be a part of the Projects Team which was involved in the development of new software Projects. It was always interesting to work on a new project which involved interacting with various departments, noting down their expectations, and giving shape to a whole new Project with exciting features and a superb User Interface (UI). Moreover, those working on the Projects were considered to be superior (a wrong perception) to the other teams.

Those who were in the Maintenance team were always busy troubleshooting and were at the beck and call of users encountering problems in the usage of the software already implemented. Moreover, it was a thankless job as the users were not always kind with their comments and feedback if the solution was not given on time. Users generally had to wait for the maintenance team to analyze, find the bug, resolve their issues and close the call. The availability of the Maintenance team was crucial and essential. The Department would lose its credibility over a while, if the bugs found were not resolved in time. Additionally, any lapses would be a heavy drain on the bottom line and would cost us heavily too. Members were unhappy that they were required to handle issues in the software projects, developed by somebody else.

The third group in the Operations setup was involved with processing various systems required for the Refinery. Their jobs involved loading tapes, running Cobol programs after changing relevant parameters, correcting the errors found, reporting, printing the reports, segregating and sending them to the departments, backing up and logging the details. They felt these jobs to be routine, keeping them busy throughout the year with no challenges whatsoever. They were disinterested as they felt they were wasting their potential and desired to move out.

As all the teams were getting frustrated and demotivated, I thought that a new way forward would be ideal to challenge their capabilities and develop each one of the team members. After discussing, brainstorming, and getting a consensus, reallocation was done. All the jobs in the Operations, Maintenance, and Projects were combined to form distinct systems, and team members were accordingly distributed to handle each system.

This ensured that projects became bug-free, and as they were maintained by the same team who had developed them, the turnaround time was reduced. Teams started finding out new ways to automate the routine jobs of the Operations, which were later on handed over to Clerical staff who were able to handle them with the least supervision. The time so gained was reused for the development of other value-added projects, compounding the value addition, which increased the efficiency and effectiveness of all team members, as well as credibility of our Department.

As the whole cycle of Development, Maintenance, and Operations of each system rested with the same team certain prerequisites were made mandatory to enable the teams to be focused on timelines and deliverables. Processing had to be carried out during the days, as was already prescribed, to enable the outputs from these to be transmitted in time as inputs for the next system. The Maintenance would assume priority, and any bug found would need to be resolved within a specific timeframe, with a proper escalation mechanism in place. Projects would be guided by timelines fixed for each project and it would be the responsibility of the team members of the particular system to abide by the respective timelines.

As a result, team members became charged to find time to work on the projects that they felt were challenging, by ensuring that the Projects were bug-free. They took initiative and efforts to automate all routine jobs of the Processing, Printing, and Back up and all processing jobs were phased out from DG Machine to PC Server-based ones by the same team. A sure 'win-win' situation for all.

Guidelines:
The following are a few of the guidelines to be implemented by the team leader, which will facilitate accountability and build trust among the team members:

- Define the duties, expectations, and description of the job and their relevance to the objectives of the organization.
- Be realistic about the timeframe and make sure the team members are aware of the deadlines for each project they take up.
- Outline the time commitment and set aside adequate time for each task.
- Give proper feedback.
- Check the progress by following up.
- Conduct regular team meetings for feedback and take inputs on the progress of projects, with soft reminders, wherever warranted.
- Listen to the needs of the team members and guide as a coach when and wherever required.
- Delegate important responsibilities according to hierarchy.

How does one become the best team leader?
The tips mentioned above are a few quick fixes that can improve the functioning of one's team in the short run, but they have no direct bearing on him becoming a better team leader. Growing oneself as an effective leader is a difficult, slow, and meticulous process, which requires both

personal and team dedication. John Maxwell in his Book [1] **'5 Levels of Leadership'** describes the journey of how a newly appointed leader can become a good team leader.

John Maxwell's Theory from the Book [1] 'The 5 Levels of Leadership':

Level 1: *Position*: Where you are placed in the 'position' of power and the only reason the team follows you is that they have to.

Level 2: *Permission*: Where a good team leader builds strong relationships with his team members such that the team tacitly gives him their 'permission' to lead them.

Level 3: *Production*: Where the leader starts using his influence and credibility to motivate the team to produce results.

Level 4: *People Development*: Where the primary goal of the leader becomes identifying and developing as many leaders as possible by investing in them and helping them grow.

This is reflected in his quote as given under,

'Successful people position themselves well. Successful leaders position other people well.' Once the leaders manage to continuously develop leaders amongst their followers, who can now train other leaders, they can achieve the fifth level.

Level 5: *Pinnacle*: Where people follow Pinnacle leaders because of who they are and what they represent.

Napolean Hill hits the nail when he says: *"It is literally true that you can succeed best and quickest by helping others to succeed."*

Fifth-level leaders are rare but leaders can strive to reach there, or at least perform at Level 4. Let us see the styles of leadership prevalent today before we go forward. Leadership can be categorized into 3 different styles, which can be tried under different circumstances.

The Commander:
Commanders make and impact most decisions. Often, such decisions may not be ideal as they may not consider all available information, alternatives, and perspectives. This style is effective in the short term when there is a major crisis to be attended to.

The Coach:
Coaches are concerned with developing people, creating and facilitating a trusting environment.

They encourage personal growth and empowers the team for long-term capabilities including leadership development. They listen and provide feedback. They make decisions collectively with the team, explaining the rationale behind the decisions. Coaching style leadership is required when the team lacks focus, expertise, and understanding of what should be done and how. This style can be tried till the team reaches the stage of 'Performing'.

The Supporter:
Supporters tend to make joint decisions with the team *as equals*, delegating the majority of decisions to the team. They are ego-less, quiet, and are concerned with the creation of harmony and balance between team members. As a facilitator, the Supporter helps to remove the barriers and coordinates the activities. Supporting style can be used at all times.

Qualities that can be developed:

To support, coach, and motivate the team members to succeed, you need to be strong, decisive, knowledgeable, supportive, cooperative, and also imbibe the following qualities.

Engage and Involve:
Great leaders convey their vision with passion, to bring unwilling employees onboard. They can get those employees who are suspicious of change, to commit to the organization and put more effort

into their work. Effective leaders support and provide the right conditions, so that the employees can give off their best and contribute to the long-term well-being of the organization. The secret lies in the leaders' ability to engage positively with teams across the organization.

Strengthen the team identity:
An effective team leader takes steps to strengthen the team identity while maintaining members' valuable differences, by reiterating the team's common goals. They revisit the team's shared goals and purpose to remind their people, that the work they were doing was vital not just to the team, but to the organization as well.

Be encouraging:
Leaders must truly care for those whom they lead. They have to be patient and drill below the surface of those they lead and encourage them. When you care for someone, you will begin to see and respect what skills they possess and mentor them. That care and respect, cause them to see you as their leader.
"If you want to lift yourself up, lift up someone else." – Booker T. Washington

Apply the *Pygmalion* principle:
The *Pygmalion* effect, or *Rosenthal* effect, is a psychological phenomenon wherein high expectations from team members lead to improved performance in a given area, and low

expectations, to the decreased performance. According to the Pygmalion effect, the targets of the expectations internalize their positive labels; those with positive labels succeed. A similar process works in the opposite direction in the case of low expectations. The idea behind the Pygmalion effect is that increasing the leader's expectations of the followers' performance, will result in better performance by them. It takes courage to go deep and extract the valuable ones from the worthless and ignore what other voices keep telling you about them. Leaders must be encouragers as they have the extraordinary power to extract the best from the oblivion into prominence.

Personal Insight
I have tried this principle innumerable times and got my team members to perform exceptionally well, even exceeding their self-perceptions about themselves, when others kept rating them low.

Encourage collaborative work:
Find as many opportunities as possible to get people to work together. Nothing builds team identity more than collaborating side by side on a challenge. It can also take the form of some extracurricular activity or a fun activity. By creating engaging activities one can get the members to take part in activities that they find interesting and valuable. For instance, defining a

team charter, developing a project schedule, or an activity list for completing a major task. Such activities will keep them focused on the team's objectives. I once got all my team members to enact a skit on 'safety', scripted and performed by all of us in the team.

Have open communications:
An effective leader can communicate effectively with others to achieve a common goal. He creates and maintains a climate of trust and open, honest communication, allows team members to talk openly with one another, promotes the exchange of feedback, and provides team members to work through misunderstandings and conflicts.

Try not to be overbearing:
Effective leaders don't enforce their dominance in group discussions but direct the outcome of group activities. They focus their attention on the setting of objectives and priorities and shaping the way the team can be aligned. They are tough, discerning people who can hold their ground in any company, yet not dominate the group.

Implant a sense of urgency:
When team members are told about the significance of their work, they try harder to reach the goals. They feel duty-bound to collaborate to meet the challenge at hand. To create a sense of urgency, impress upon the team how its work would solve a serious problem or benefit the company.

Provide compelling directions:
It's the leader's job to make it clear what the members are supposed to be doing together. Unless a leader articulates a clear and compelling direction, there is a real risk that different members may pursue different agendas.

Recognize contributions and skills:
Find opportunities to recognize the skills and contributions of individual team members and explain how their efforts have helped the team progress toward its goals. This will make team members feel valued and appreciated, which will further strengthen their commitment to the group.

Empower:
The leader should empower the team members to have sufficient authority to act and make decisions. At the same time, he should clarify and set clear boundaries.

Recognize the value of team differences:
Publicly acknowledge the value of differences of the team members, and explain how those differences can synergize to realizing the team's common goal.

Be flexible:
The leader should be flexible enough to allow team members to adapt to changing conditions including the outside environment as well as

within the team itself. He should help them to adjust and manage change.

Bond the Team:
Teams that work together harmoniously are better and more productive than teams that don't. Create opportunities for members to know one another. Members need to know who is on the team and who is not and remain bonded. The leader should create situations to make them bond, back them up, recognize and support them, even in their absence. Don't ever rebuke them in public.

Be mature emotionally:
There is no one right way to set a particular direction as the same is emotionally demanding because it always involves the exercise of authority. This inevitably spawns agony and doubt for both the person exercising it and the people at the receiving end. Emotionally mature leaders can tackle such situations and move forward by establishing a clear, challenging team direction without conflicts.

"There is no such thing as a self-made man. You will reach your goals only with the help of others." – George Shinn

Let's now move on to the next important segment of teamwork- **Roles, Responsibilities, and Relationships of Team members** in the next chapter, as the members play the key role in executing the teamwork and taking the team to the next level.

Chapter 3

ROLES, RESPONSIBILITIES, RELATIONSHIPS

"One piece of log creates a small fire, adequate to warm you up, add just a few more pieces to blast an immense bonfire, large enough to warm up your entire circle of friends; needless to say that individuality counts but teamwork dynamites." – Jin Kwon"

Clarity of Roles, Responsibilities, and Relationships

The key to tapping into the potential synergy of a team is with proper delegation of tasks, based on various strengths of its members. There should be total clarity in roles and responsibilities, and the team needs to be cohesive enough in creating strong relationships with one another.

Every team member should have clarity on the following, should seek clarification, and get a copy of the documents on Organization Structure, Role, Job Description, Accountabilities, Resources, Tools and Equipment, Qualifications, etc.

Roles

Roles need to be well-defined and appropriate, well-matched, complementary, comprehensive, and should cover everything that needs to be accomplished with proper responsibility and accountability.

Team members, as we've understood, are a group of people who work together to achieve a common goal. They exist together for a purpose or task and are mutually accountable to achieve the same. There would be multiple roles within a team. I would like to refer to the description of team roles as determined by *Dr. Meredith Belbin.*

Belbin Team Roles[*2]:
Dr. Raymond Meredith Belbin is an English researcher and management consultant best known for his work on management teams. Dr. Belbin has found an answer to the question of why some teams are successful while others are failing as he concluded his research spanning for more than 9 years.

As per his findings, successful teams comprised of members with diverse and compatible roles, while unsuccessful ones were characterized by constant conflicts between members with similar tendencies and personalities.

Belbin Team Roles[*2]:
Belbin presented conclusions from his work after studying how members in the teams interacted during the exercises and business games run at Henley Management College in the book[*2]
'Management of Teams: Why they succeed or fail?' His experiments proved that good teams required *a balance*. Recognizing that the strongest teams have a diversity of characters and personality types, Belbin defined nine possible team roles. They were intended to describe and foresee the potential success of management teams. Each team role defined by Belbin comes with its own set of characteristics, strengths, and weaknesses, which he further categorized into three groups.

Action-Oriented Roles:
Action-oriented roles focus on improving the team's performance, acting on the ideas, and meeting deadlines. The three action-oriented roles are:

Shaper –Who questions the assumptions and is an extrovert.

Implementer – Who brings self-discipline to the team.

Completer Finisher – Who pays attention to the smallest details and makes sure that things are done right.

People-Oriented Roles:
People-oriented roles bring people and ideas together. The three people-oriented roles are:
Coordinator – Who brings order into the team.
Team worker – Who provides support to the team in a diplomatic manner.
Resource Investigator – Who develops external contacts.

Thought-Oriented Roles:
Thought-oriented roles analyze options and provide technical expertise. The three brainy roles are:
Plant – Who comes up with innovative, ground-breaking solutions.
Monitor evaluator – Who assesses team decisions analytically and critically.
Specialist – Who is an expert in a particular subject matter.

Dr. Belbin wanted to see how teams made of people with similar personalities function in the everyday business environment, and how they cope when it comes to problem-solving. To achieve this, he again divided the examinees into four groups based on their personalities, viz., *Stable Extroverts, Anxious Extroverts, Stable Introverts, and Anxious Introverts.* Looking at these groups, one can decide where any team member is likely to fit.

After his research and experimentation and on further analysis, Belbin concluded that every 'pure' team that achieved a noticeable result had one thing in common: one of the members had taken the role of an **Implementer**.

These Implementers were:
- Disciplined individuals who got their work done swiftly and systematically;
- Tough-minded, practical, trusting, and tolerant towards others;
- Conscientious and aware of external obligations;
- Respectful of existing conditions and ways of looking at things;
- With a well-developed sense of self-image and a high degree of internal control;
- Interested in working for the company, and were not in pursuit of self-interest;
- Ones who could identify with the mission of the organization and would accept and look for goals that fell in line with its ideals and aspirations;
- Practical and realistic;
- Ones who did not evade the job because they did not like it, or it did not interest them.

Belbin figured out that he finally found the secret sauce for the perfect worker. Therefore, the next logical experiment was to create a team made entirely out of Implementers.

Just like with the Apollo team we saw earlier, the expectations were high. And just like with the Apollo team, these teams of 'perfect workers' also were a failure. According to the conclusions, they also produced average results. Implementers were well organized and meticulous but lacked any real ideas. They were strongly committed to anything they started but became uncomfortable when plans changed. Though they worked well, they failed to get good results.

This leads us to conclude that successful teams comprise members with different but compatible roles. The team roles describe a pattern of behavior that characterizes one person's behavior in relationship to another in facilitating the progress of a team. This approach enables an individual or a team to benefit from knowing oneself and adjusting his/their behavior to the demands being made by the external situation.

It may be noted that the tool helps to describe an individual's 'preferred' team roles and is designed to indicate how one would ideally operate in a team environment. Strength in one team role is often at the expense of what might be seen as a weakness in another context.

Meredith Belbin's explanation of his team roles method allows readers to benefit from his extensive experience of its use in practice. Numerous real-world case studies are shown in the book[*2] on how to apply the theory in real situations.

"Great things in business are never done by one person; they're done by a team of people." —so spoke *Steve Jobs* and how true it is when you watch successful teams perform well. Let us now see the next ingredient for effective working of teams.

Responsibilities

Shared Responsibility:
Shared Responsibility allows team members to feel equally responsible for the performance of the team as a whole and its outcome. It permits individuals to have primary roles for completing the team tasks and remain flexible to do what is necessary to accomplish the team's overall goals and tasks.

Be an effective team member:
To become an effective team member besides sharing the responsibility for overall performance, as well as responsibility related to one's given task, one has to follow certain guidelines as mentioned below: -

Participate:
A team member should participate fully and keep up with the commitments. To fully participate, one needs to contribute ideas, ask questions, challenge conventional ways of doing things, and

complete all tasks assigned to him in a timely and professional manner. Without enthusiastic participation by all team members, a team will just remain a gathering of individuals. The unique ideas, skills, perspectives, and viewpoints one brings to the team are crucial for the successful completion of tasks.

Listen intently to understand and share:
A team member should *listen* and *share* information. He should work at understanding what others are saying, ask them to repeat and clarify, if not understood, paraphrase what was heard, and query if it was heard correctly. Listening to what other team members have to say is one of the most vital skills one can ever contribute to a productive team atmosphere. One should always be willing to give an attentive ear to the views of other team members and expect them to do likewise. The members should also share information and ideas.

Cooperate and execute:
A team member should be ready to work towards achieving the common purpose, accept and agree on the team goals, establish and work on the tasks (be it new or revised) to be completed. He should execute as per the project plan, monitor progress, achieve the milestones declared, interpret results, and complete the project or task assigned to him.

Communicate:
The members should share their thoughts, opinions, and feelings without fear. If one has a problem with someone in the group, one needs to talk to him about it. Letting bad feelings grow would only make one sour, and the member would want to isolate himself from the group. When in doubt, one needs to ask questions and get clarifications for the same. If an idea or a task isn't clear, collective responsibility demands that appropriate questions are asked and the matter got clarified.

Be supportive:
Team members should be supportive of one another to achieve the results. They should be open to ideas and support the contribution of others.

Recognize and appreciate:
A member should give and receive positive feedback, as well as recognize and appreciate the contributions of all other members so that, that will reinforce one's behavior, build esteem, and enhance a feeling of value and accomplishment.

Be productive:
Members should be committed to high standards of quality and be optimally productive. All members should be responsible and accountable to be effective and contributive. They should hold

each other accountable and strive for continual improvement.

Demonstrate reliability and flexibility:
A team member should be reliable at all times and never let down the team. He should be flexible and be ready to step in when another member has any issues in delivery.

Stay humble, hungry, and smart:
It's time we changed the way we prepared people for success, says Patrick Lancing in his ted talk[*3.] Drawing from personal observations, he makes a compelling case that, in our increasingly team-oriented world, the key to success is ***staying humble, hungry, and smart***. He argued that if a team player had these 3 simple virtues, he would become an excellent team player. An ideal team player has to be *humble* by putting others ahead of him, which simply means that he should not be arrogant or egocentric. Similarly, he should also be hungry and ambitious to get more work done, work hard at setting high standards, and not confine himself to doing just the minimum. He should also be *smart* and intelligent. If you miss any one of these virtues, you may fall into the category of an *accidental mess maker,* (not smart), *a lovable slacker* (not hungry,) or a *skillful politician* (not humble) like a Chameleon.

Let us now move on to the next ingredient for effective working of teams:

Relationships

Solid relationships:
Solid relationships are based on trust, mutual respect for one another, understanding one another, sincerity in all aspects, respect for contribution, acceptance of differences, and mutual accountability. The objective is not to become the best of friends, but to know how to work together and support one another. By being solid, relationships can tolerate conflicts, misunderstandings, disagreements, and occasional bad days. Positive relationships will be inclusive and will involve the contributions of each of the team members. Diversity will be encouraged. Team members will be prepared to listen and give feedback without fear and negative vibes.

To attain solid relationships, we need to improve the rapport amongst the team members by adhering to the following behaviors: -

Don't blame others:
Pointing the finger at someone for problems will only make one look weak. It is better to own up and take corrective actions.

Support the group:
Support your team members' ideas as generally, people support a person who supports and helps others.

Be a mentor:
Listen actively, look in the eyes of the person speaking to you, nod, ask inquisitive questions, and acknowledge what's heard by paraphrasing the same; also, seek others to paraphrase what they have heard.

Get involved:
Take time to help your fellow teammates. If you've helped them in the past, they'll be more than happy to lend a helping hand when you need it.

Share feelings:
Openly share feelings, and ideas for a deeper understanding of one another. Discuss one's strengths and weaknesses.

Speak with clarity:
Speak with clarity. It, along with respectful dialogues, ensures a better understanding of one another. Be prepared to elaborate and give illustrations. Repeat and restate statements to ensure correct input receptivity. Ask for confirmation from others for having heard you correctly.

Seek and accept help:
Seek and accept help from others. Members listen to and are open to others' ideas and viewpoints. Request others to be sincere and honest in their feedback.

Provide feedback to others:
Take a confirmation that others are ready to receive your feedback. And then share your views with them. Give positive feedback when others have been helpful to you.

Contribute to team's awareness:
Call attention to what is happening in the group. Invite others to give feedback, feelings, and their perceptions of what is happening.

Resolve problems:
Contribute to defining problems and identifying their root causes. Suggest ways to diagnose and identify what is hindering the team in detecting the problems. Enhance team productivity by offering alternative ways of reaching group goals.

Be creative:
Be attentive to suggest ways in which one can support one another in the team. From time to time, take on various roles and functions to increase the team cohesiveness.

Use diagnostic approach:
Use the ability to understand why and how certain things happen, by using a diagnostic approach.

Case study

We had started the Voice Over IP (VOIP) system first time in the BORL refinery in the year 2009. It was the first time that IP telephones were going to be installed in a Petroleum-based industry in India. So my team was super excited about it.

The top management used to assemble for coordination meetings once a week, and we decided to take the opportunity to demonstrate the aforesaid at one of the regular coordination meetings. I informed the members of the meeting that the Voice Over IP system configured for the Refinery will be demonstrated in the coordination meeting on such and such a date.

Our team along with the System Integrator arrived at the meeting room the previous evening and configured the demonstration set up and tested to see that everything worked perfectly well. We had set up 3 IP phones inside the meeting room and connected them to the *Call Manager* (The exchange for IP system), which were powered from another room occupied by a Senior Manager sitting close by. The demonstration was to start immediately after the coordination meeting was over. As the meeting got over, I got up and started the demonstration by trying to call on one of the IP phones configured. Unfortunately, the call did not go through and I was a bit alarmed and surprised, as it had been tested and was working perfectly the previous night. Not knowing what had happened I looked around.

On seeing my plight, the team members got up and rushed out of the room to check. They realized that the power supply to the call manager had been switched off. To not lose face, I continued explaining the features and benefits of the new system, as well as what all features we were going to demonstrate and establish in front of the coordination committee team members. After some time, keeping the members engrossed, I once again tried to make the call, and fortunately, it got connected. One of the members took the phone and people talked and tried many of the features of the new IP phones, based on my explanation. My team members were missing when our Team was lauded and appreciated for putting up such a technologically advanced system, and that too at a remote location in such a short time.

Later, I was told about what had taken place. The occupant of the room from where our power supply had been taken had switched off the supply, locked the room, and left for attending the coordination meeting. Our team members had rushed to the room but were unable to get the room opened. They then had rushed to the receptionist, borrowed the spare key, opened the room, and restored the power supply, while I was speaking at the venue. As a result, they could not be present there and missed the limelight, when the team got applauded for its efforts and a very successful demonstration.

I am ever indebted to my team members who rose to the occasion and saved my face and saved the day. Come to think of it, there have been many such occasions when the team displayed its spirit and did more than what was expected, or far beyond the members' assigned duties. These were live examples of team cohesiveness and bonding, where the successful completion of a job meant more than individual greatness. The team demonstrated beyond doubt, the concept of mutual accountability and shared responsibility on such occasions.

This quotation by Phil Jackson appropriately sums up the role of team members in increasing the effectiveness of teams.

"The strength of the team is each individual member. The strength of each member is the team."

How do we form a great team?
In addition to working towards a common purpose or common goal, with an effective leader and effective team members, great teams are characterized by some other traits as well. Moreover, they operate based on certain common principles and strategies. So let us now move on

and find out what makes a **team effective** and what makes it dysfunctional, in the next chapter.

Chapter 4

TEAM EFFECTIVENESS

"No one can whistle a symphony. It takes a whole orchestra to play it." – H.E. Leacock

What exactly is an effective team?
- Team effectiveness refers to the system of getting people in a company or institution to work together effectively.
- An effective team has some **characteristic**s that allow the team members to function more efficiently and productively.
- They develop certain **behaviors** like sharing leadership roles and have methods to share accountability for their work products.
- They operate on certain **principles** of shifting the emphasis from a single individual to several individuals within a team.
- They also have certain **strategies** in place which help them achieve superlative performance.

Why Build an effective team?
Building and maintaining effective teams is a time-consuming and complex process particularly in businesses where the pressures

on time are often too high as every project is supposed to be done on yesterday basis. Most efforts at building an effective team don't work, as managers and staff are far too busy. They fail to appreciate the time and effort that need to be invested and the attention to detail that is required to be put in. However, there is no doubt that teamwork contributes highly to set up an inspired team, improve productivity, enhance morale, and reduce costs. Teams will transcend through previous steps and become disciplined, self-reliant, self-organized, and effective after experiencing victories and failures, growing and gaining experience together.

- **Characteristics, Principles, and Strategies that can make a team highly effective:**
  Let us now look at the attributes or characteristics of a team and team members, the operating principles and strategies which come into play and form a major part in making or breaking a team.

Characteristics
A team's essential discipline comes from the following characteristics:

- **A meaningful common purpose or goal that the team has given shape to:**

Most teams respond to an initial directive or a project or an assignment received by them from outside the team. But to be successful, the team has to take the onus of this or own this goal or purpose, and give shape to it. They should develop it and work for accomplishing it within the timelines decided.

- **Specific performance goals that flow from the common purpose:**
  Once the common purpose is identified, the key performance goals and key responsibility areas should be identified. Compelling goals will inspire and challenge a team to deliver within the time, as well as give it a sense of urgency. Members will also be required to focus on the collective effort necessary to accomplish it, rather than harping on any differences in title or status.

- **A strong commitment to executing the work:**
  Teams must agree on who will do what jobs and by when. They also need to agree and decide on the schedules, as well as how the decisions will be taken and modified. In an effective team, each member including the leader will do an equivalent amount of real work without shirking or slackening pace and contribute in concrete ways to the team's collective output.

- **A mix of complementary skills:**

These include technical or functional expertise, problem-solving skills, decision-making skills, and interpersonal skills. Successful teams rarely have all the needed skills at the outset. They develop them as they work based on the challenges that they encounter as they execute the tasks.

- **Mutual accountability:**
  Trust and commitment cannot be forced on anyone. In an effective team, by agreeing upon appropriate goals and committing themselves to deliver the same without fail, the teams establish their accountability to one another and not just to the leader.

Once the essential discipline has been established, a team is free to concentrate on the critical challenges it faces.

Principles
The following are the principles based on which a high-performing team operates for effective performance. Their behaviors also will be consistent with the same.

- **A clear, elevating goal**:
  The team has a compelling vision, a strong sense of purpose, and a common set of values, and clear goals.

- **Clarity**

The team members have an understanding of the purpose of the team, expected outcomes, their roles, responsibilities, and expectations.

- **Result-driven structure**:
  It will be amazing to find how much you can accomplish when it doesn't matter who gets the credit and all work towards attaining the common goal in a structured manner with the focus only on delivering the results.

- **Competent team members**:
  A motivated and confident team doesn't need formal leaders. The team makes most decisions. Any member could step in and become a leader in specific areas and situations. People on such teams tend to be highly competent, committed, and self-driven.

- **Unified commitment**:
  Team members have a high degree of commitment to the team's mission and one another. The team schedules the work and commits to the time allocated for it.

- **Collaborative climate**:
  Team members share information and ideas and are open to the ideas of others. They have an understanding of how to work together and use the resources effectively to achieve the goals. The members avoid winning or looking good at the expense of others.

- **Applying the principle of Ubuntu:**
"*In Africa, there is a concept known as **Ubuntu** – the profound sense that we are human only through the humanity of others; that if we are to accomplish anything in this world it will in equal measure be due to the work and achievements of others,*" said Nelson Mandela

Let me narrate a story to explain this principle. An anthropologist was waiting for transportation to the airport when some children gathered around him. To entertain them, he put some sweets in a basket under a tree about 100 yards away from where the children were, and they were told to race and pick them up. They were informed that the first one to get to the basket would win all the candy for themselves.

Once the anthropologist gave the signal the children took each other's hands and ran together to the tree. Once there, they sat in a circle and shared the candy. The surprised anthropologist asked them why they all went together when one of them could have had all of the candy for himself/herself.

One of the younger girls looked up at him and said, "How can we be happy if all the others are sad?"

Africans use the term "*Ubuntu*" to describe what this girl believed. Ubuntu simply means "*I am, because we are*". If this principle can be adopted, any team can do wonders. Just for a moment, imagine the power of teams and organizations practicing Ubuntu. Is it not a complete and powerful game-changer?

- **Shared standards of excellence**:
  The team develops tangible work products and the members are mutually accountable for the same.

- **External support and recognition**:
  Team members are supportive of one another to achieve the results and each one supports the contribution of others.

- **Principled Leadership:**
  Team members share leadership roles and develop their scope of work.

- **Communication:**
  Team members are committed to positive communication practices, including active listening, sharing, and giving and receiving feedback. All these will be covered in detail in Chapter 7 on communication.

- **Capability:**

Team members have the necessary skills and knowledge to complete the tasks efficiently and appropriately.

- **Continuous Improvement:**
  Team members are committed to continuously improving work processes and team effectiveness.

- **Creativity:**
  Conditions that encourage diverse thinking, new ideas, and innovative solutions are always supported and put into practice, resulting in the generation of more and more creative ideas.

As the saying goes, "There is no 'I' in Team! And that is the secret of success of the team!"

Let us now see the strategies of for ensuring Team effectiveness:

Strategies

Strategies to improve team effectiveness:
The task of building better teams and improving their effectiveness entails four simple steps, viz.,
1) Clarifying one's Team Mission
2) Setting Team Goals
3) Creating A Plan
4) Conducting Progress Reviews.

Clarify your team mission:

Make sure that the mission you develop for the team is the team's reason for its existence or being or its purpose! For example, if your team is responsible for developing new products, your mission could be to create innovative products that will make the client's life easier and more enjoyable, or develop a software to help in controlling the cost or say develop a service that will save money for the client. Every team should have definite objectives or goals.

Setting up team goals:
There are some guidelines for setting up the team goals. The goals should support the team's mission or purpose. Goals should specify an end date. They should be measurable. For example, instead of saying we want to increase production this month, a specific quantity should be spelled out. To illustrate, a measurable goal may be: this month we will increase the production by fifteen percent over last month's production.

Create a plan:
A team plan is simply a written blueprint for the team's envisaged success. It spells out the team's mission, outlines the team's goals, and lays out a strategy for fulfilling the mission and the goals. It states the responsibilities of each person on the team, what they do and how they do it. It should spell what each person should do and how he or she will be accountable for the same.

Conduct progress reviews:
These are meetings where the team members assemble to discuss the team's results and the way ahead.

Items to be covered in team progress review:
- Check to make sure the team is effectively accomplishing its mission.
- Review the team's goals and make necessary adjustments. This is a great time to keep the team goals out in front of everyone.
- Set a date for the next Review.
- Review the team plan and determine if any updates or changes are required to be made to make the team more effective. Talk about the things that are working well and discuss what areas need to be improved.
- Reiterate the responsibilities of each team member and the actions they need to take next.

Dysfunctional Teams
An organization is indeed a huge team of people working towards a common goal! However, though it looks simple, a team is a dynamic system that needs to be managed well due to the complexities of the group dynamics involved.

Why do some teams struggle?
There is a possibility that you may be having a team or teams that are dysfunctional, or may

not be performing as required. Let us now delve into the reasons for teams becoming ineffective and struggling to deliver.

Selfish team members:
Most of the time the dysfunctional teams are those with members who are individually more concerned about themselves and their gains at the expense of the goals and gains of the team. They care only about themselves and care for others only if they know that they could gain something in return. Such selfish team members sabotage what a team is capable of achieving.

Lack of Vision:
A team will not be able to align themselves for success if a clear purpose or vision is absent. Everybody will move in different directions if they don't know why they are working together and make incongruent assumptions. Even if you start a project with a clear vision and the team members interpret it differently, then the vision will get disarrayed.

Unclear Roles:
If you don't know what exactly you are supposed to do or if roles are not clear, you will struggle to decide what to do next. This leads team members to focus on some very primary tasks under the notion that they are being productive, albeit, in reality, they will be wasting their time. Without clearly laid out

roles and expectations for each team member, they may take on a task that does not suit their experience and expertise, which will again be a sure recipe for failure.

Poor decision making:
Most teams miss out on coming up with a good approach for decision-making and fail in two areas. The first is when they overthink decisions and waste a lot of time in the decision-making process. This de facto leads to not deciding at all.
The second is when they don't spend enough time thinking through the decisions they make and as a result get into the implementation and thrash mode, only to give up later or come out bruised and wounded.

Rigid mindset:
Many teams fail to grow or inspire due to their rigid mindset. Most of them fail because they have already assumed that they cannot improve, change, or re-frame their situation. This often means that the smartest or the most technical of the teams might get stagnated at some spot.
Some teams can jump to the conclusion that if they can't solve a particular issue quickly using their standard approach, there is no solution.

Lack of resources:
Lack of enough or appropriate resources is at times one of the major killers of a team as a

whole. Sometimes this is the team's fault, but most often the first culprit is the organization that chartered the team in the first place. Not having the right tools, authority, and equipment will lead to a dip in the team morale and eventually, its commitment will also start to wane.

Poor dynamics:
Mutual respect amongst the members is a must for any team to achieve results and maintain cohesion. Team members need to interact constructively. It is not enough to be an expert in one's field. What's required to get the team dynamics right on track is to be an expert in communicating with fellow team members effectively.

Lack of trust:
If team members distrust one another or make inroads into other's work territories, they cannot achieve results. Team members must feel a sense of loyalty to the team as well as to one another.

Patrick Lancing in his book *'The five dysfunctions of a team'*4'* has brought out how the lack of trust leads to other dysfunctions analogous to the collapse of a pack of cards. The first dysfunction, of course, is the **absence of trust** among team members. Essentially, this arises from their reluctance to be susceptible to an error within the group. Team members who are not genuinely open with one another about their flaws and faults make it difficult to build a foundation for trust. This failure to build trust is damaging because it sets the tone for the second dysfunction which is the fear of having conflicts.

Fear of conflict:
Teams that lack trust are incapable of engaging in an unfiltered and worthwhile debate on ideas. Instead, they resort to covert discussions and guarded comments aimed at avoiding conflicts, which is not a healthy sign in the long run.

Lack of commitment:
Team members seldom commit to decisions taken as they have not put forward their opinions in the course of open debates, though they may pretend to have agreed to them during meetings. Because of this lack of real commitment and buy-ins, the team members become dysfunctional.

Avoidance of accountability:
Without committing to a clear plan of action, even the most focused and ambitious people hesitate to discuss an activity that is beheld as counterproductive. Failure to hold one another accountable thus creates an environment that could become the breeding ground for the fifth dysfunctional factor.

Inattention to results:

This occurs when team members put their individual needs such as ego, career development, recognition, or even the needs of their divisions above the collective goals of the team. Thus, like a chain, with just one link broken, the entire teamwork crumbles if even a single impaired functioning is *left unattended*.

Now, let me list down certain other reasons for the teams turning dysfunctional. These are generally those that are taken care of by effective teams. I have also included a few reasons listed by The *Ken Blanchard Companies* in their research on unfolding the causes for the teams failing to reach their potential.

- Lack of a sufficient charter
- Unsure of what requires a team effort
- Lack of effective and/or shared leadership
- Lack of planning
- Lack of management support
- Lack of focus on creativity and excellence
- Lack of training
- Lack of interpersonal communication skills
- Absence of systematic problem-solving skills
- Inadequate or nil planning
- Improper goal setting or unclear goals
- Inability to deal with or fear of conflicts, including the absence of a collaborative conflict resolution mechanism.
- Absence of group decision-making skills
- Poor management of meetings

- Lack of collective focus
- Not performing together but performing individually
- Complaining, selfishness, inconsistency, a sense of complacence

A saying by *Helen Keller* is apt and worth quoting here.
"Alone we can do so little, together we can do so much"

Once we have understood each of the above cardinal principles and other factors required for team effectiveness, or what should be shunned, what is now required is to put them into practice. There needs to be some system, procedures, or documented process, which should be binding on all team members and which should be adhered to by each member. This leads us to the next chapter on how we can become an **Incredible team** by imbibing whatever we have learnt till now.

Chapter 5

HOW TO BE INCREDIBLES

"The way a team plays as a whole determines its success. You may have the greatest bunch of individual stars in the world, but if they don't play together, the club won't be worth a dime." – Babe Ruth

Key Areas for Effectiveness

Key Areas for Teams to become effective:
Teams can continuously improve their effectiveness by focusing on their functioning in five key areas: Goals, Leadership, Roles, Relationships, and Procedures,
•**Goals**: What the team aspires to achieve (covered in Chapter 1).
•**Leadership**: How the leader supports the team in achieving results (covered in Chapter 2).
•**Roles**: The part each member plays in achieving the team goals (covered in Chapter 3).
•**Relationships**: How the team members get along with one another (covered in Chapter 3.)

- **Procedures**: The approach, method, or the process framework that helps the team conduct its work together. This will be covered in this chapter.

Focusing on effective procedures or effective processes are important investments for your team's productivity. You don't want people to be reinventing the wheel every time they take up a new project or assignment. It is not only inefficient, but it also increases the likelihood that the project or the effort won't be successful.

Let us now get into some basics before we go further.

The Stages of Team Formation:

Team formation takes time and usually follows some facile stages, as the team voyages from being an assemblage of strangers to becoming a coherent whole with a common goal.

Psychologist Bruce Tuckman first came up with the memorable words: **'forming, storming, norming, and performing'** in 1965 to describe the evolutionary path to high-performance that most teams follow. Later, he added a fifth stage that he called **"adjourning"** for wrapping up the project. Here, I would like to reframe and call the final stage **Out-performing or Skyrocketing**, where the team continues to deliver **incredible** results.

Let us go deeper and find out the different stages of team formation.

Forming:
Teams initially go through a stage in which the members are generally *positive* and *polite,* a few members are anxious, and a few are excited as they haven't yet worked out exactly what work the team was expected to perform. The roles and responsibilities of members are not clear. This initial stage of formation is usually short, where people are introduced to one another and discuss the modalities of teamwork.

Storming:
At this stage, decisions don't come easily as the team members vie for positions and they try to establish themselves with other team members and the leader. Clarity of purpose may increase but with plenty of uncertainties. Reality sets in and one's authority may also be challenged as the positions and roles are clarified.

As the details of working get elucidated, some members feel overwhelmed by the quantum of jobs to be done, some become uncomfortable with the approach used, some react by questioning the worthiness of the goal and some resist taking on tasks. This is the stage when many teams can fail.

Norming:

Agreement and consensus are largely formed within the team and they respond well to the facilitation by the leader. Roles and responsibilities are clear and accepted. Decisions are made by group consensus. A few decisions may be delegated to individuals or small teams within the group. Commitment and unity are strong. The team may engage in fun and social activities. The team discusses and develops its processes and working style. There may be general respect for the leader and some of the leadership roles are shared by the team members.

Performing:
The team is more strategically aware, as the members now know clearly what they are doing and why. They have a shared vision and can stand on their own feet with no interference or participation from the leader. The team has a high degree of autonomy. Disagreements occur but now they are resolved within the team positively and necessary changes to processes and the structure are made by the team. The team can work towards achieving its goal. They deal with the relationship, style, and process issues along the way. Team members look after one another. The team members require delegated tasks and projects from the leader as they no longer need to be instructed or assisted. Members might ask for assistance from the leader about personal and interpersonal development. The leader delegates and oversees what is working well in the team,

what needs improvement, and how it can make the changes required

Effective Procedures / Processes

Out-performing or Skyrocketing Stage:
This is the stage when the teams go beyond just performing, they rise to all occasions without fail, and put in an outstanding performance on all fronts through trust, bonding, sharing, and vibrant group dynamics, *thereby becoming incredible* teams.

• At this stage, templates and forms are created for automating the team's ***regular tasks*** and projects. Detailing is done as it is extremely important to guard against getting caught on the wrong foot. One needs to preempt situations wherein a staff member introduces any amount of variability in the templates.

• Every time you get caught in an anomaly or a ***breakdown***, the same is dissected, root-cause analyzed, and a definite process put in place to avoid such lapses in the future. Brainstorming with team members is done and the issues that caused the breakdown are discussed rather than pulling up the person who has caused the issue. Team members contribute without any fear, facilitating accurate analysis, proper steps for preventing the same in the future, and better record keeping.

- For all **projects** taken up by the team members, regular meetings with agendas, Minutes, and action plans are put in place, by referring to the respective templates.

- For jobs taken up on an ad hoc basis due to an *emergency*, teams are expected to log the same for the creation of a proper database to enable quick attention and solution to such eventualities.

- **Knowledge sharing** is encouraged to ensure that reinventing the wheel is avoided after attending to any breakdown/ emergency, or after implementing a unique project.

While we need to have definite processes, it's also wise to accept suggestions for refining them as we go along. This will ensure that they continue to improve over time. This not only ensures consensus but also commitment and shared accountability by the team members.

Case study:
During the late 1990s, the dispatch facilities at Bharat Petroleum Refinery were expected to run 24 * 7 hours, which could not afford any downtime as that would tantamount to loss in billions to the Corporation. Any failure of the Network / PCs / Printers / Servers or the Software had to be attended to immediately.

As the dispatch activities had to be carried out all through the night, we had deputed Service Engineers to attend to normal routine issues in the night and to ensure that computer systems and networks run without any hitches. At a point in time, we noticed that the Service Engineers were unable to solve the issues, and the engineers from our department were being called almost regularly in the night to resolve the breakdowns. This resulted in discontent and frustration as we were unable to identify what was going wrong.

We did a thorough analysis and realized that the new servers were failing intermittently. We called the vendor who supplied them as they were expected to provide 99.9 percent uptime. We did not accept his explanation. Eventually after a series of discussions, we could convince him to supply a redundant server for changeover and to provide service without any downtime, that too at no cost to the Corporation.

The regular logs helped us in pinpointing the issues, the timings of failures, the root cause analysis filed by us, and the gap in the promises or terms and conditions, and actual deliverables. We put a proper process in place, guidelines, and escalation mechanism to take care of possible eventualities in the future, paving the way for satisfaction to all the stakeholders.

Process for making team decisions:
A consensus decision is taken when there is a difference of opinion on any issue.

Types of decisions can be categorized as minority, majority, unanimous, or consensus decisions. **Consensus** is in finding a proposal to be acceptable enough, that all members can support it, and no one opposes it. Consensus doesn't mean a unanimous vote or a majority vote but everyone involved is totally satisfied. It requires time and active participation by all the members. Consensus connotes the involvement by the group of individuals in their governance and other activities to exert influence.

Processes during team development:
Several processes are involved in the development of teams. We need to formalize the routines, roles, and norms that improve effectiveness We should also formalize shared mental models about resources, goals, responsibilities, and build the competence of the team. During the team formation, we need to develop cohesion and bonding within the team and inspire the members to think of themselves as members of one family, and part of one social identity.

During the storming stage, with all of the probable power struggles listed, the teams may go astray. They need to focus on their goals and avoid becoming distracted by any relationships and emotional issues. Cohesion and bonding will help in easing the issues.

Processes for developing cohesion and bonding:

Cohesion is a state in which the members are enjoined to bond, which links them to one another or the whole group. Cohesive teams don't happen overnight. It takes time and diligence to achieve them. Cohesion stems basically from the attraction developed to a group or a task, and the desire to remain a member of the group, which is a sequel to both cognitive and emotional processes. Cohesion increases when the members are like-minded, teams are smaller, and the members interact frequently with one another. Team networks with a high degree of cohesion provides a free stream of information and build trust and sharing amongst the team members, which facilitate the overall performance.

Cohesion is generally beneficial as it triggers more motivation and members are more than willing to share information. Better interpersonal relationships exist within the team and it's easier to resolve conflicts effectively. As team norms are aligned to organizational norms, cohesion ensures better performance too.

Cohesion can be harmful if team norms are inconsistent with the organizational norms. Moreover, you have to be very careful as there is a real danger of teams becoming over-cohesive and susceptible to groupthink, as team members stop debating, to 'protect' the group, and where, over time, their shared beliefs and assumptions become wrong, unless and until challenged by someone.

Therefore, while cohesion is crucial for high-performance teamwork, it has to be carefully managed and regularly moderated by the input of ideas from outside sources. Many methods for bonding with the team members and making them cohesive are elaborated in the section 'The Journey to Effective and Higher Performance' given below

Processes for Building Trust:
Trust refers to positive expectations of another person in situations involving risk.

Trust is based on emotional bonds and mutual understanding and is generally present in highly effective teams. Trust is the foundation of real teamwork. And a failure on the part of team members to understand and open up to one another stems from their unwillingness to be vulnerable within the group. Great teams do not hold back one another. They admit their mistakes, their weaknesses, and their concerns without fear of reprisal, and not only build trust in one another but also seek help and encourage the team members to provide help to one another. To build trust, teams should be encouraged to share their fears and vulnerabilities by having several meetings, fun games, and off-site engagements.

Create standard processes:
The approach, method, and procedures to achieve incredible results should be well defined. The process needs to be straightforward, well defined, designed, discussed, documented, and continuously improved to gain cooperation from all team members. It's not just about how the team gets things done, but also how it thinks as a whole. All processes need to be mastered, mapped, documented with revision dates, adhered to, and changed when required. The un-optimized processes are time-wasters and backsliding on productivity.

Effectively these documents are binding like a contract which all team members are required to adhere to. These are developed based on expectations that each team has on its members, and all are expected to abide by that contract. It is designed and tailor-made specifically for a given team to meet the specific needs of its members. Each team member needs to input, and this is a chance for all members to voice their opinions and the member is accountable for the statements in the agreement.

Issues that may generally arise like effective communication methods, participation by all members, decision-making, problem-solving approaches, management of conflict and differences, responsibilities and conduct, project management, and so on based on the general expectations from each team find a place here.

Clear procedures need to be documented and mapped as teamwork guidelines, to be complied with and followed by all. This is just an example and more could be added based on the nature of teams.

- Team-working agreement
- Effective communication
- Project management
- Effective meeting procedures
- Root cause analysis
- Solving problems
- Making decisions
- Conflict management
- Completing tasks
- Planning
- Managing change
- Evaluating performance
- Skills required and to be developed
- Budget

Few Samples are given below:

Team-working agreement
- Every member is responsible for the team's progress and success

- Attend all team meetings and be on time
- Listen to and show respect for the views of other members
- Criticize ideas, not persons
- Expect and accept constructive feedback
- Resolve conflicts constructively
- Always strive for win-win situations
- Avoid destructive behavior
- Ask questions when you do not understand

Effective communication (to be covered in <u>Chapter 7</u>):
- Communicate openly and supportively
- Listen openly
- Interpret nonverbal messages
- Give useful feedback
- Receive feedback effectively

Project Management:
- Start with consensus on project goals like say, the goal of Project A.
- Then work to a project plan, specify all milestones with the responsibility and expected date for completion.
- PERT Charts
- Indicate Key Responsibility Areas with the responsible person and the date of the deadline.
- Indicate disputable points and points that depend upon outside of the team resources and so on.

- Testing/ Inspection/ Site Visit/ Demonstration/ ……. Details/ Dates/KRAs/Responsible Persons/ ….

Meeting Guidelines: (sample only)
- Project meetings will be held every Monday.
- Meetings will be called by the team leader.
- Meetings will begin and end on time.
- Decisions will be made by consensus or majority votes.
- The role of the scribe will be rotating.
- Minutes will be issued by e-mail within 24 hours of each meeting.
- Exceptions are not allowed.

Conflict Management (covered in <u>Chapter 6</u>)

Skills required and to be developed:
- *Key teamwork skills required in the interpersonal space are* trust and acceptance, communication skills, collaborative problem-solving skills, and conflict resolution skills
- *Key teamwork skills required in the self-management space are* setting goals, self-motivation, time management, and effectiveness.
- *Key teamwork skills required in the Project management space are* goal setting, planning, task coordination, project

management, and performance management.

Case Study

We implemented Unified Communications for a campus spread over 3000 acres at Bharat Oman Refineries Limited at BINA, M.P. and Crude Oil Terminal (COT) at Vadinar, Gujarat with 86 km of OFC and 33 km of UTP cable in Ring topology interconnecting more than 70 buildings, enabling 600 + data and voice endpoints. We also implemented IP Telephony for voice communication along with Collaboration tools and Video Surveillance. We have stored all documents electronically right from the day of inception and are world record holders for the fastest implementation of SAP. Security, Wireless LAN, WAN, and other high-tech technologies were implemented with the capability of pushing 3 GBPS of Data, Voice, and Video on the same network making BORL the first Smart Digital Refinery at a remote site like BINA.

To handle such a huge site, a simple drawing to track progress with a sample tracker sheet as shown was prepared. The staff involved had developed further detailing sheets. This is just to indicate how we could track a mammoth job with a team comprising of just 6 team members. It also shows how we could get all stakeholders and all team members to be aligned to work in the same direction, release work fronts, provide work permits, and in general help to execute within the timelines and the budget

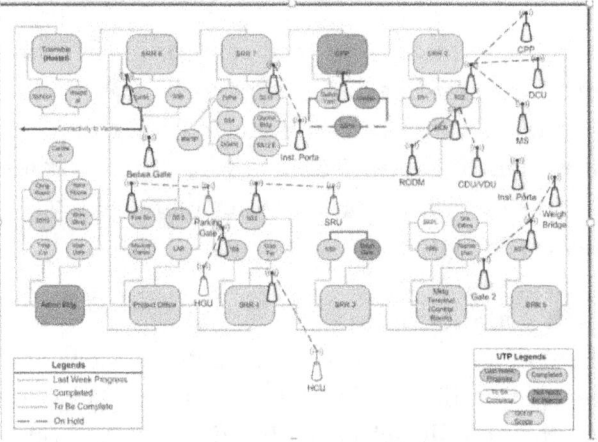

Sample drawing for Tracking overall progress with color-coding for taking action

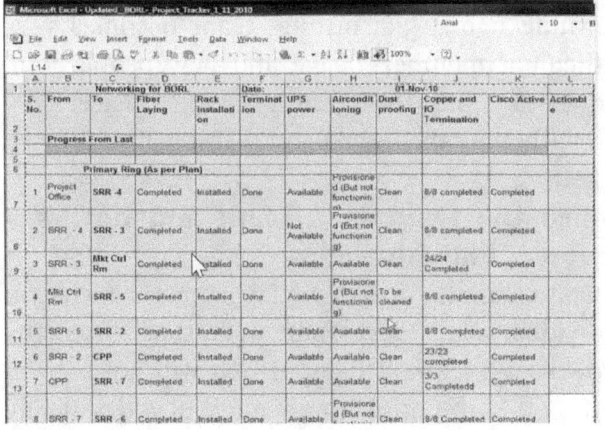

Sample Tracking sheet for high-level monitoring, status updates, and reporting

The Journey to Incredible Performance

All teams are unique and multifaceted living beings. Extraordinary performance is a journey, a predictable advancement from a group of individuals to team members, who begin to think in terms of "we, us, ours" rather than "you, your, yours, I, me, mine "and so on.

Form a stable team
When a team is formed, we should focus our attention on the stable stage. We should take our time to carefully select team members. And once done, we should stick with them through thick and thin.

If everything goes smoothly, it may take about six months to create a high-performing team. Forming a high-performing team becomes very difficult if members leave and new people join. However, improvement takes place by strengthening the inter-team relationship.

Coach the team as a team and not as a group of individuals:
Usually, human resource departments focus on individual skill development, rather than the growth of a team. This approach will not help in getting a high-performing team, but a drastically

inferior high-performing group. So efforts should be taken to coach the team members together on different behaviors expected of them, with role-plays and gamification to engage all team members.

Rearrange office seating:
Encourage interaction amongst the members and create opportunities for social conversations by rearranging the office seating. Set desks so that everyone can see one another; choose an office that suits the size of the team. If it's too small, it'll be cramped and uncomfortable and if it's too big, the distance between members may discourage interaction.

Get them out of their work desks:
Stimulate interactions amongst team members in places other than their desks as well. We had a common pantry where we used to assemble to get our tea and snacks. It can also be around a water cooler, in a kitchen next to the coffee maker, or a lounge area. Casual talks and a relaxed atmosphere provides incentives for the flow of great ideas and increased team cohesion.

Bond over media such as books, movies:
Ideally, we can find common ground between people and help them communicate among themselves through the medium of Books/ Movies/ Songs / Magazines/ Quiz/ Surveys which

will be a good point for shared experiences and discussions.

Take the team out of the office occasionally: organize a picnic, a party or a simple team lunch, or any other social event like a team sport, a get together with family members, and just let them bond. Work-related topics will come up sooner or later, and the relaxed atmosphere will encourage everyone to give their input on the subject discussed, whether it is useful or not. Somewhere amidst those suggestions, there may occur a solution our team had been looking for.

Engaging team in creative pursuits:
To achieve satisfaction on different levels within the organization, employees should be empowered to be creative, intuitive, thorough, and generous by encouraging them to produce Newsletters, Bulletins, In-house magazines, and organize small events to celebrate. Such events were always organized in our departments facilitating bonding and cohesion.

Monitoring and maintaining consistency

Effective working procedures:
Ineffective procedures will prevent the team from becoming high-performing one, and can cause problems in gathering, organizing, and evaluating information, while at the same time they will discourage creativity, innovation, and risk-taking.

A constant vigil to ensure that effective procedures are in place will prove beneficial in the long run.

Shared values:
All members of a high-performing team share goals, objectives, and values while being focused on results and solutions. For excellence to become a habit, you need to not just define a shared approach to working together, but also need to practice it over and over until it becomes second nature.

Complementary abilities:
Builders can provide you with the walls, but the house won't be functional if plumbers, electricians, or carpenters are not involved. So also in teams, each member possesses a certain knowledge, a set of skills, and personal strengths. Synergy with other members is what makes the team highly productive. This needs to be emphasized enough so that the team members appreciate and value the contributions of other members.

Shared leadership:
Depending on the task the team is working on, different members take turns in stepping into the shoes of the leader. When a few undertake a job on which they excel, the expert leads them by giving instructions, while all others support in other ways. As the leader is an expert in the field,

others will follow his orders and instructions, no questions asked. This will change when expertise is required in another area and a suitable candidate steps in. Even though there is a formal team leader, his thrust would be on coaching, mentoring, and ensuring that all the required procedures are followed and the output delivered is excellent.

Adaptability to changes:
Projects change all the time. When it comes to handling drastic changes, high-performance teams don't revel in self-pity and give up. They analyze, adapt, put in a proper process to handle and perform.

Constant learning and improving:
Mistakes are a learning opportunity and there are no repercussions if members examine what went wrong, learn from it, and resolve not to commit the same mistake again. They may knock down the wrong walls, but the important part is that they won't do it again.

Regular result evaluation:
To ensure that a project is heading in the right direction, an engineer has to take a step back and look at the project from time to time. A high-performing team does that after every major milestone is achieved, as it gives it a realistic completion time, as well as an opportunity to foresee obstacles that may arise in the future.

Case study:
Incident Reporting & Investigation System (IRIS)
I had the privilege of developing a software application with virtual teams for the fire and safety department of Bina Refinery.

It may be noted that I had two new trainee engineers located physically in Mumbai and two engineers at Bina, the remote location where this Application had to be implemented. We had a period of only three months to implement such a massive Application system that could register incidents and track the investigation till action is taken and closed to prevent or avoid such mishaps in the future.

Even though the requirement is quite huge, let me give briefly the requirement of the Application in a few sentences. Accidents can happen at any plant due to unsafe acts or unsafe conditions. There could be many factors leading to the same. If an accident occurs, then it has to be investigated and a first investigation report (or FIR) is to be prepared after the victim is moved to safer locations or after he is hospitalized. Even if no human being was involved, an FIR has to be prepared and submitted to the statutory authorities. This needs to be verified and approved by a hierarchy of role holders. Any major fatal accidents may have a bearing on the operation of the plant too.

Once the coordination committee sees the report, a team comprising people from different departments, based on nature/ severity and type of accident, is formed which is expected to conduct a visit to the site, inspect, interview, and accordingly prepare the investigation report. Based on different meetings and approvals, an action to be taken report is also generated. Depending on the nature and severity of the accident, department representatives are deputed to take action. Till this is completed, it remains as an entry in the 'Action to be taken Register'. The role holder is accordingly intimated and reminded till all jobs are completed

The Strategy

In the case discussed here, the roles and responsibilities were earmarked, as per which the 2 engineers at Bina would collect all information to develop the Application and explain the requirements in a regular 20 minutes daily meeting. They will also check the manual records being maintained at Bina, scan the same and intimate the 4-member team regularly. The role holders at Bina would develop the routines for master data and user interface to capture the data from the users and populate the relevant masters as well as get the modules tested by the role holders at Bina. The role holders in Mumbai would develop the routines for processing as well as integrating the modules and relevant reports. As the roles and responsibilities were clearly earmarked, the development and testing also took a fast pace and was implemented on a fast track basis within less than three months, surpassing all expectations the user department had from this small team.

Value Additions

This workflow-based application was complete in all respects and had end to end modules for tracking all types of incidents, for all categories of staff/personnel, reporting status of all recommendations, tracking actions taken by departments, including sending automated reminder mails to all those who had defaulted in taking relevant actions. This was developed in-house within three months and was estimated to cost more than 8 million USD if the same was to be outsourced.

All requirements as given by the F&S department of BORL were incorporated and customized to suit the BORL IRIS system

It could be observed that all principles highlighted above such as shared leadership, mutual accountability, utilizing complementary skills present within the team, and learning and improving, worked well for this team. Despite being managed virtually from different locations; it went on to become a highly successful project with the stakeholders not wanting to even try another Application from outside.

Giving negative feedback

Negative feedback should be provided in private and not in public and it should be timely so that the team member concerned has sufficient time to change his behavior and give better results next time. Having a one-on-one meeting regularly with team members is also beneficial in the long run. These could be used to discuss an individual's habits and behaviors and how they could impact the team. However, these discussions should be held in such a way that no other members can eavesdrop.

Provide thoughtful feedback on small but important things, like the way the individual in question faces other members, or how much they interrupt others, and how well they listen to, and so on.

All said and done, the fact that you as a leader need to set an example for the behaviors you expect from others can hardly be overstated. For that, you should know your failings and work on them. Your team will respond well to such behaviors and are more likely to follow your lead. It may also happen that they may not appreciate your remarks and may confront you. That could lead to stress and conflict, and other repercussions. However, the most important thing to remember is that you should attempt to change the team members only after exhausting all other choices.

"If everyone is moving forward together, then success takes care of itself." --Henry Ford

Forming a high-performing team takes time and effort, but once they jell and start producing results, they become an indispensable asset of every company. However, the players being human beings, there will be room for some conflicts to develop either between the leader and members or inter se amongst the team members. For more on that, let us proceed to the next chapter on conflicts and their **resolution**

Chapter 6

CONFLICT RESOLUTION

"It takes two flints to make a fire." -- Louisa May Alcott

Conflict Resolution:
Resolution of conflict plays a major role when working together. Strength lies in the differences and not in the similarities. One of the major differences between an average team and a high-performance team is the capability of the latter to handle conflict in a constructive manner. People normally tend to fear and avoid conflict. They believe that conflict does not belong to the workplace. However, dynamic organizations use conflict as a creative force. Diverse views help improve thinking, learning, and overall performance. Hence, instead of viewing conflict as a negative trait, a high-performance team views it as a strength of the collective group.

About conflict:

First, let us understand what conflict is all about. Conflict develops because we are dealing with people's lives, jobs, children, pride, self-concept, power, self-esteem, ego, and sense of mission or purpose. Conflict arises due to differences in power, values, and attitudes of individuals. When they come together in teams, their differences result in the creation of conflict as individuals or groups are not getting what they want when they are seeking their self-interest. It can be noticed that conflict occurs because of poor communication, seeking power and authority, dissatisfaction with the style of management, weak leadership, lack of openness, and change in leadership at any level.

Conflict indicators:
Early indicators of conflict can be recognized. You can know that there is conflict when you observe one's body language. Other indicators are when there are disagreements regardless of issues and when people withhold bad news. Increased lack of respect, open disagreements, and display of and desire for power are other indicators of the presence of conflict. The controversies usually relate to changes sought in the way one has always done things, notions of fundamental values, determined and stringent advocates for either side, inability to compromise, rampant rumors, threats of retaliation, conflicts in the value system, lack of clear goals, and so on.

Dealing with conflict:
Conflict is the most difficult parameter to deal with both personally and professionally. Albeit inevitable, conflict can be minimized, diverted, and resolved. There are strategies available for resolution which do work. Any conflicts that surface must be depersonalized and dealt with early, either between individuals or within the collective team.

Why is conflict essential?
Conflicts can improve team performance if managed collaboratively. They foster a deeper understanding of issues and an exchange of information that facilitates problem-solving, decision-making, and generating new ideas.

To avoid the negative consequences that can come up from frequent disagreements, most methods of resolving conflict, stresses the importance of dealing with disputes quickly and openly. When managed properly, conflict is not necessarily destructive. It can result in significant benefits for a team.

Conflict is destructive when it:
Takes attention away from other important activities, undermines morale or self-concept, polarizes people and groups, reduces cooperation, increases or sharpens difference, leads to irresponsible and harmful behavior such as fighting, name-calling, and so on. Conflicts within a team can take numerous forms from tensions

and arguments to an unwillingness to support one another. Left unresolved, such conflicts can destroy a team's ability to progress toward its goals.

How can one avoid this scenario and bring a conflict to resolution? Let us discuss a few steps.

Techniques for avoiding and/or resolving conflict:

As it is always better to meet conflict head-on, plan and communicate that frequently. Be honest about concerns and agree to disagree. Understanding healthy disagreements will facilitate better decisions. Discuss differences in values openly. Continually stress the importance of the following policy and do communicate honestly.

Follow these guidelines for reaching a consensus:

Avoid arguing over individual ranking or position. Present your point as logically as possible. Avoid "win-lose" statements. Discard the notion that someone must win. Avoid changing of minds only to avoid conflict and to achieve harmony.

Treat differences of opinion as indicative of incomplete sharing of relevant information and keep asking questions. Keep the attitude that holding different views is both natural and healthy to team building.

Conflicts within the team and how to handle them:

When we say that there is a conflict within the team, we do not mean a superficial quarrel. It is suggestive of deep-rooted misunderstandings that are capable of breaking the team into unamendable pieces, costing the company money and manpower. Let us discuss how to prevent and manage destructive conflict which is bound to happen in any team sooner or later. When conflicted parties start attacking the person(s) concerned, rather than the problem per se, then do take prompt action as the constructive conflict is sure to turn into a destructive one.

Define the root cause of the conflict:

When conflict arises in one's team, we need to ask ourselves why the team members are arguing with one another, check whether there is a deeper personality conflict involved and if any member was becoming stubborn or not. It is worthwhile to check whether the individual concerned insisted on getting his way or not. Answers to these questions will help one uncover the root cause of the conflict as to whether it's a behavioral or a situational problem.

Negotiate a resolution:

Avoid dictating a resolution to the conflict. Instead, negotiate a solution that everyone involved can agree and live with. Point out the importance of agreeing on certain issues. Remind people that if one member bullies the rest of the team into accepting his or her viewpoint, the rest of the members would resent that person and not support this decision. Encourage members to find common ground and explore new possibilities.

Encourage active listening:
During discussions designed to resolve a conflict, team members must learn to become active listeners. That is, they must be prepared to restate points made by a speaker, demonstrate that they've understood what the speaker was saying, control any behavior that suggests a lack of interest in the speaker.

Ask questions that encourage a speaker to expand his or her points with further information or lines of reasoning, refer back to points made earlier and build on those ideas, get the speakers to explain the reasons behind their opinions, if necessary, remind team members that each person has the right to offer his or her ideas and solutions to problems without interruption and that they should be able to finish their thoughts even if one or more members disagree.

Often, there isn't just one right answer to a conflict or problem. A team needs to consider a broad range of possible solutions before feeling confident that it has selected the best one. Withholding angry feelings will only lead to resentment. Letting everyone constructively share his or her frustrations will let the team move on to solutions. It has to be remembered that one of the reasons a team is created is to get varying opinions on how to solve problems. Allowing people with different perspectives and skills to air their ideas without interruption is one good way to gather more functional views.

Remind team members to forgive:
Once your team has resolved a conflict, remind people not to nurse any sort of ill feelings towards anyone in the team. Let them remember that forgiveness is not a sign of weakness; rather it is a sign of maturity and high emotional intelligence. It further enables people to let go of any remnants of anger left over from the past conflict milieu. Thereby they will make sure that such dysfunctional feelings will not taint and vitiate future interactions within the team.

Approaches to deal with conflict

Avoiding (We both lose):
This is probably the worst approach to handling conflict because it boils down to avoiding conflict altogether, i.e., pretend that it does not exist. Fundamentally, this unassertive and stubborn approach benefits nobody as none of the parties concerned get what they want. Individuals who

use this approach tend to accept decisions and requests made by their bosses without questioning, and often delegate difficult decisions and tasks if they ever find themselves in a position of power. This passive approach perhaps may be useful on rare occasions, but better it be avoided.

Accommodating (You win, I lose):
While avoidance is a proclivity to keep the status quo, *accommodating* is a strategy to satiating the needs of others, even if it means you lose. You are ready to give up what can be yours legitimately. Individuals who lean toward this sacrificial approach tend to be either very indulgent or have high empathy. *The accommodating* approach can be useful in certain circumstances but eventually, it would turn out to be very ineffective.

Compromising (Nobody wins, nobody loses):
By compromising, you may not win but may get to resolve the conflict quickly, without losing much. This approach necessitates both sides to give up something so that they can gain something else but usually, nobody is happy with what they get. This approach is beneficial in certain situations and is used as a strategy for negotiating.

Competing (I win, you lose):

Unlike *accommodating*, with the *competing* approach you take a firm stand on the issue on hand and do your best to get your way. You can do this because you are in a position of power to get what you want, or by using strong arguments or even by bullying. Individuals who use this approach are generally influential and enjoy a lot of credibility within the company. They may also be stubborn and loud and may see each conflict as a battle for supremacy. They can as well be very aggressive during discussions.

Although this technique is excellent when you want your team to make urgent and hasty decisions, this approach has its share of faults too. You may also become unpopular.

Collaborating (We both win):
Collaborating approach is the high point of conflict handling, being both assertive and cooperative. It requires a high emotional intelligence of all participants and their willingness to come up with unique win-win solutions. However, this type of solution demands emotional detachment and rational thinking and would take time; it is seldom achievable during intense conflicts. Therefore, *collaborating* is somewhat difficult to realize.

Collaboration is inarguably an ideal means for bringing together the knowledge, experience, and skills of multiple team members to contribute to the development of a new service or product more effectively than the individual team members could. It involves a commitment to a shared goal and interdependence that comes from the understanding that what is accomplished together is greater than what could be realized individually.

Collaboration calls for a discipline that requires an understanding of the practices that could make it successful.

There are official tests that can help you determine your (or your team members') behavior in conflict situations. It will give you an insight into the way you handle conflict and which areas you need to strengthen to become a conflict management expert.

Case Study:

This happened at a time when I was handling the full operation of the Computer Systems Department. There was an instance when the software used at the Dispatch gantry which was expected to operate 24 * 7 to prevent any loss of revenue to the Corporation failed due to some bug in the system. The correction was to be done by the maintenance team at the Head office which was about 15 KMs away from the refinery. After rectification, the executable files were to be brought to the Refinery in floppies and installed on the Servers at the Refinery. It may be worthwhile to note that the WAN and Internet facilities were unknown during those days. The installation was to be carried out by a senior staff in my department who alone had the login credentials.

The refinery timings were based on factory timings which were from 7.45 AM to 4.15 PM and the timings at the head office from 9.30 AM to 5.30 PM when the formal working hours would be over. The staff working in general shift usually left for the day at 4.15 PM. As the said bug came to light late in the afternoon, we were required to stay back and attend to the breakdown and release the system before we left for the day.

The bug had to be found, analyzed, corrected, tested, and the revised software had to be brought from head office and implemented at Refinery. Knowing fully well that the solution would be received after 4.30 PM only, I asked the Senior staff to wait for the arrival of the officer from the head office. He was not prepared to wait and adduced that the office timings were over. And said that if the officer did not arrive by 4.15 PM, he would leave. This resulted in a conflict as he was not willing to budge. I asked him to pass on the login credentials to me. As he was sure that we will not be able to handle the situation on our own, he passed on the same to me and left. I requested the junior staff reporting to him to stay back, as I did not want to be bulldozed into accepting this behavior and wait till the next day to resolve this issue.

Once the officer from the head office arrived, we three together got into the operation of getting the system to rework. It took us more time to resolve, than it would have taken under normal conditions, as the three of us were not at home with all the routines as the Senior officer was. However, finally, we could get back the system in operation and release the same and leave for the day.

The next morning when the Senior officer walked in, he was expecting us all to be a worried lot and beg him to attend to the issue. He was surprised and taken aback to see that everything was normalized. Now, having realized that we were strong enough to take care, execute and that he was dispensable, he relented.

After that, proactively he took out the list of all pending activities and without any prodding got all the issues resolved by staying back and doing the extra bit that was required. I got a written appreciation from the stakeholders, as they had not expected such a change in deliverables from that day onwards. What was almost an "I Win, You Lose" situation turned around into an "I Win, You Win and We All Win" situation for all. Here, what saved the day was the determination and grit shown by us and the faith in team leadership. A few additional processes were also put in place to preempt such eventualities in the future.

Resolving the conflict
The best kind of conflict is a productive one. However, if your team is unable to maintain constructive conflict, preventing confrontation altogether would be the next best move to make. As you have seen from the case study, by managing conflicts skillfully one can:
- gain cooperation from team members,
- improve performance and productivity,
- reduce stress and preserve the integrity,
- improve relationships and teamwork,
- increase staff morale, and
- increase the credibility of the team in the eyes of stakeholders.

Overall, it is a complicated but highly rewarding skill, which will boost your team's morale and productivity to a whole new level. Keeping the conflict in the mind for a long time and becoming bitter over it will be counterproductive. So forgive and forget as said by Jean-Francois Cope

"I invite everyone to choose forgiveness rather than division, teamwork over personal ambition." --

Conflict management is an essential part of becoming a high-performance team. But how do you negotiate and/or resolve conflict unless you are good at communicating? So now let us talk about the best skill required to be effective in a team, which is the **communication** skills at the workplace.

Chapter 7

COMMUNICATION

"To effectively communicate, we must realize that we are all different in the way we perceive the world and use this understanding as a guide to our communication with others." **Anthony Robbins**

Excellent Communication:
Communication is where leadership lives and breathes. *"An effective team is characterized by trust, conflict management, commitment, accountability, outcome focus. All possible with great communication."* — Cam Lee.

As a boss, you are constantly advising, informing, explaining, discussing, reviewing, counseling, suggesting, persuading, convincing, coaching, guiding, humoring, and responding.

So your message must always convey both your vision and the organization's purpose and values, whether it be in the spoken or written communication.

What people fail to appreciate is that the message conveyed is not only about what you say, but also about how you say it. When a person sends or receives information, ideas, and feelings with/from others he not only uses spoken or written communication but also nonverbal communication.

If effective procedures are the foundation of an effective team, communication is its roof and all team members must take it seriously and improve on the same. Excellent communication is the glue that holds the team together, which is also the means to extract cooperation from all members.

What should be communicated?
We must communicate about the organization's strategy, speed, direction, and results openly with employees so that they understand, embrace and align themselves to the company's strategic direction. Communication within the team should be clear, concise, honest, timely, consistent, and accurate.
.
By having frequent direct contact with your employees, listening to what they say, and having honest two-way communication with them, you are far more likely to be the boss they deserve, respect, and trust. And you are far more likely to identify issues before they become problems and solve problems before they become crises.

How is it be delivered?
Of all the responsibilities of leadership, particularly during challenging times, communication is the most powerful and enduring one. How we communicate orally or in writing has more impact than the words we choose. Since human beings are intuitive, we constantly read and react to nonverbal cues. As aspiring leaders, we need to be aware at all times of what we are projecting to others, whether they see us as confident and optimistic or tentative and worried.

Open Communication:
The key to team performance is the open communication that happens in teams, which means that the focus is on coaching rather than on directing. Open lines of communication provide motivation, maintains interest, and promote cooperation at all times. It allows the team to coordinate shared roles, provide feedback, clarify details, and resolve conflicts effectively as well as address issues openly and candidly.

Effective Communication:
The attributes of a great leader include his self-awareness of what he knows and what he doesn't know. Many problems in organizations can be avoided if the leaders communicate clearly. Often others assume that we understand what they are talking about, but the truth is far from that.

Effective oral and written communication should be clear, brief, and concise.

It is important that each team member feels comfortable speaking his/her mind about his/her responsibilities on a project. This will allow for the expression of creative ideas and ensure that questions are asked and mistakes avoided. Regular group meetings and emails should keep everyone up to date on the progress being made and new developments in teams.

It is always a good idea to assume nothing. Remember to communicate at the level of your audience. It is also critical to check if your message has been understood or not. Many problems can be avoided by simply checking for understanding. For smaller interactions just asking if the message has been understood or not and for larger ones, sending out a survey can help in getting a proper response.

Communication within high-performing teams requires the free flow of information, a shared agreement that no topic is off-limits, and frequent and respectful interactions among team members and other individuals in the organization.

Poor communication is destructive:
Poor communication can result in poor quality, missed deadlines, and low morale. Teams rely on effective communication to pool their work efforts. When team members communicate

poorly, a team is exposed to several negative consequences.

Poor communication can cause interpersonal conflicts in the form of personal attacks, sarcasm, and arguing. It can also cause the members to interrupt, talk over one another during meetings, remain silent, hint at problems but do not address them, false consensus where everyone nods in agreement but does not agree.

Perhaps the most destructive consequence of poor communication is difficulty in reaching an informed decision. When team members withhold information or attack one another's ideas, the ability to generate creative solutions to problems is stifled, resulting in bad decisions. Teams can't work towards their goals if members don't communicate constructively. If you've diagnosed communication problems in your team, you need to take action quickly.

The following measures can help.

Create a governance mechanism for touchy discussions:
Acknowledge to your team that argumentative conversations will inevitably happen as members work out solutions to problems, make decisions, and explore ideas. The question isn't whether contentiousness will arise or not, but

how your team will deal with it when it does take place.

Constructive conflicts also happen between team members but they are mostly personal and organizational. It is important to realize that misunderstandings can be a good thing too because they prevent groupthink. We need to define rules with inputs taken from team members about how to discuss contentious issues. Whenever necessary, revisit the rules and remind team members to follow the same.

The rules which teams develop may vary from team to team, but the following are basic ones applicable to all teams: Recognize another person's idea, even if you don't approve of it. Wait for the other person to finish speaking without interrupting. If you disagree with someone, explain the reasons behind your stand.

Keeping the peace between people:
You can't change a person but you can always try to keep the peace between people to let them see each other's strengths so that they will work together. There will always be people whose differing personalities would be such that they don't see eye to eye. Helping them to see each other's strengths will encourage them to work together more productively.

Invite views from team members:
In any team, you can observe a few people dominating the discussions and others remaining quieter. The team loses out on valuable input from all members and the longer they work together; more members may get rooted in such demeanors. It is necessary to take steps to ensure that all members contribute their views and ideas during team discussions and meetings. Here also establishing proper communication norms can help.

If you notice someone remaining silent during a discussion, invite him or her to provide input. You can also insist and ensure that team members provide input one at a time during the meetings.

Use meeting time wisely:
Insist that everyone be acquainted with the agenda and read all necessary information before coming for a meeting. During meetings, the focus should be on resolving problems rather than on information sharing unless it is a part of the agenda. Steer it back to items on the agenda if you find that the discussion was going off track. Discussing new initiatives and sharing knowledge at the end of the meetings will motivate the teams.

Focus people's attention on team goals:
Talking about goals helps team members to remain focused and direct their attention away from interpersonal conflicts or other distractions.

To improve communication, revisit the team's initial purpose periodically.

Write frequent progress reports to be distributed to all team members. When people see their progress in writing, they'll be motivated to communicate about the team's effort in a focused way. I used to circulate the same in spreadsheets after each meeting where progress on each task after the last meeting is informed. A sample os shown here

Focus on issues and behavior, and not on character:

Encourage team members to express their anger or frustration in terms of issues or other people's behavior, rather than on their character. Insist that people use "I" language to describe the impact of another person's behavior on oneself rather than "you" language.

Pay attention.

Give the speaker your complete attention. Show that you're listening. You must be 'seen to be listening. Our life experiences and beliefs can sometimes mislead us. Keep an open mind and do give feedback. Try not to interrupt and do respond appropriately. Active listening encourages mutual respect.

Written Communication Skills:
Time is often the biggest barrier to effective communication. People in a business setting tend to focus on completing tasks quickly and their written communication suffers as a result. Remember that haste is a waste. Taking care to be *clear, cohesive, complete, concise, and concrete* when communicating will help improve our speaking and writing.

The concept that communication is the effective exchange of meaning or understanding applies to both formal and informal communication. It applies to communication up, down, and across the organization.

Everyone in the organization is accountable for the effectiveness of his/her communication. More so for when you manage others. A leader's words and actions can help employees feel safe, support them to cope emotionally, and put their experience into a context where they can draw meaning from it. Leaders must give people what they need, when they need it, communicate clearly and frequently, maintain transparency, and help people make sense of all that has happened.

Here is an apt quote on why communication goes wrong   and it leads to, be it in the family or at the workplace

"Any problem, big or small, within a family, always seems to start with bad communication. Someone isn't listening." Emma Thompson

Chapter 8

CONCLUSION

***"Talent wins' games, but teamwork and intelligence win championships."** – Michael Jordan*

High-performance team characteristics generally comprise a combination of purpose and goals, talents, skills, performance ethics, incentives, motivation, efficacy, leadership, conflict resolution, communication skills, power, empowerment, and norms, and standards.

'A successful team is a group of many hands but one mind.' said *Bill Bethel*

In life, everyone has an individual goal that they want to achieve but when you're in a team what is more important is the team's goal. When we work as a team, it's very important to set aside our pride and ego and work towards achieving the team goals. In this process, we will also be able to achieve our individual goals like improving our game, career progression, learning a new process, and so on.

Key takeaways *from the previous chapters are as follows:*

Chapter 1 - Common Purpose

High-performing teams are synergistic social units and they have a common purpose or goal or mission with shared values. They work towards the achievement of a common goal which may either be short-term or long-term. They demonstrate total commitment to the work and each other.

Chapter 2 - Effective Leadership

Leaders of high-performing teams ensure that the team remains cohesive and delivers exceptional results as per the decided timelines. Effective leaders are flexible, service-oriented, and task-driven.

Qualities that can be developed to become an effective team leader to support, coach, and motivate the team members to succeed are to: be strong, decisive, and knowledgeable. In addition to being supportive and cooperative, imbibe the following attributes: engage and involve the team, strengthen the team identity, be encouraging, apply the *Pygmalion* principle, encourage collaborative work, have open communication, try not to be overbearing, implant a sense of urgency, provide compelling directions, recognize contributions and skills, empower the team, recognize the value of team differences, be flexible, bond the team and be emotionally mature.

Chapter 3 - Roles and Responsibilities

There should be total clarity on roles and responsibilities, and the team needs to be cohesive enough to create strong relationships between one another.

The top qualities of effective team players are that they strive to achieve the overall common purpose, are mutually accountable, demonstrate reliability, listen actively, communicate constructively, function as active participants, share openly and willingly, cooperate and pitch in to help, exhibit flexibility, work as systematic problem-solvers, treat others in a respectful and supportive manner, show commitment to the team, are adept at conflict resolution, know how to put people together to work, are humble, smart, and hungry to achieve.

Chapter 4 - Team Effectiveness

Team effectiveness refers to the system of getting people in a company or institution to work together effectively.

- An effective team has certain **characteristic**s that allow its members to function more efficiently and productively. They develop certain **behaviors** like sharing leadership roles and have methods to share accountability for their work products. They have a meaningful **common purpose** or goal that the team has given shape to, specific performance goals that flow from the common purpose, a mix of complementary skills, a strong commitment to executing the work, and mutual accountability.

- They operate on certain **principles** of shifting the emphasis from the individual to several individuals within the team. A few of them being: a clear, elevating goal, clarity, result-driven structure, competent team members, unified commitment, collaborative climate, applying the principle of Ubuntu, shared standards of excellence, external support and recognitions, principled leadership, capability, communication, creativity, and continuous improvement.
- They also go by certain **strategies** put in place which makes them attain superlative performance. The task of building better teams and improving their effectiveness entails four simple steps of i) clarifying one's Team Mission, ii) setting Team Goals, iii) creating a Plan, and iv) conducting Progress Reviews.
- It can be noted that lack of the aforesaid can tilt the balance and make a team dysfunctional. To avoid such fiascos, we need to make sure that the team identifies and monitors the group's performance in a few key areas like being of a high level of trust, managing conflicts, total commitment, high accountability, and being results-focused.

Chapter5 - How to be Incredible

There are few things which we can do if we want our team to become an **Out-performing** or an **Incredible Team:**

- This is the stage when teams go beyond performing by rising to all occasions without fail and putting in an outstanding performance at all instances through trust, bonding, sharing, group dynamics, and thereby becom*ing* *incredible* teams.

- At this stage, templates and forms are created for automating the team's **regular tasks** and projects. Every time one gets caught in an anomaly, or a **breakdown**, the same is dissected, root-cause analysis done and a definite process put in place to avoid such lapses in the future. For all **projects** taken up by the team, regular meetings with agendas, minutes, and action plans are put in place by referring to the templates developed for this purpose. For unusual jobs done under an **emergency**, the teams are expected to log the same to create a proper database to facilitate quick attention and solution to such eventualities in the future.

- **Knowledge sharing** is encouraged to ensure that reinventing the wheel is avoided after attending to any breakdown/ emergency, or after implementing a unique project.

- In addition to the above the following can further help in making the team cohesive, forming a stable team, coaching the team as a team and not as a group of individuals, getting the members out of their workspaces, bonding over media such as books & movies, getting one's team out of the office, engaging the team in creative pursuits, etc.

- Maintain and monitor for consistency by having effective working procedures. It is proven that the foundation upon which an effective high-performance team is built is having effective working procedures, shared values, shared leadership, complementary abilities, adaptability to changes, constant learning and improving, and regular evaluation of results.

- It is very important to note that negative feedback is provided only in private and not in public and it should be given pronto so that the team member has sufficient time to change his behavior and give better results next time. The leader and the members should have an abundance mentality to shower praise in public and criticize in private only.

Chapter6 - Conflict Resolution

Resolution of conflict plays a major role when working together. Strength lies more in the differences and not in the similarities. One of the major differences between an average team and a high-performance team is the capability to handle conflicts in a constructive manner. Conflict develops because we are dealing with people's lives, jobs, children, pride, self-concept, power, self-esteem, ego, and a sense of mission or purpose and due to differences in power, values, and attitudes of individuals.

Conflict is the most difficult parameter to deal with both personally and professionally. Even though inevitable, conflict can be minimized, diverted, and resolved. Any conflict that surfaces must be depersonalized and dealt with, either between individuals or among the collective team.

It is always better to meet conflict head-on. So plan and communicate that frequently. Be honest about concerns and agree to disagree. Define the root cause of the conflict, negotiate a resolution, encourage active listening, and remind team members to forgive.

One of the best approaches for resolving a conflict is **collaborating** where both concerned parties *could turn winners. A collaborati*ve approach is the pinnacle of conflict handling, being both assertive and cooperative. It requires the high emotional intelligence of all participants and their willingness to come up with unique win-win solutions.

Chapter7 - Communication

Communication is where leadership lives and breathes. As a boss, you are constantly advising, informing, explaining, discussing, reviewing, counseling, suggesting, persuading, convincing, coaching, guiding, humoring, and responding.

So your message must always convey both your vision and the organization's purpose and values, whether it be in the spoken or written communication.

By having frequent and direct contact with your employees, listening to what they say, and having honest two-way communication with them, you are far more likely to be the boss they deserve, respect, and trust. And you are far more likely to identify issues before they become problems and solve problems before they become crises.

Open lines of communication provide motivation, maintains interest, and promote cooperation at all times. It allows the team to coordinate shared roles, provide feedback, clarify details and resolve conflicts effectively, and address issues openly and candidly. The most destructive consequence of poor communication is difficulty in reaching an informed decision.

The following measures can help in effective communication. Create a governance mechanism for touchy discussions, invite views from team members, keep the peace between people, use meeting time wisely, focus people's attention on team goals, listen intently, and pay attention.

Taking care to be *clear, cohesive, complete, concise, and concrete* when communicating will improve our speaking and writing skills.

Everyone in the organization is accountable for the effectiveness of their communication. This is especially true for those who manage others. A leader's words and actions can help employees feel safe, support them to cope emotionally, and put their experience into a context where they can draw meaning from it. Leaders must give people what they need when they need it, communicate clearly and frequently, maintain transparency, and help them make sense of all that is happening.

"Individually, we are one drop. Together, we are an ocean." – *Ryunosuke Satoro*

As a final word, once you become part of a high-performing team, going back to work with an ineffective team becomes a punishment.

Gita Ramachandran

May I ask you for a small favor?

I would like to thank you for taking out time to read this book I totally appreciate our gesture and hope this has not disappointed you in any way. I hope that you got at least few actionable insights that will have a positive impact on our day to day life.

Can I ask for 30 seconds more of your time?
I'd love it if you could leave a review about the book. Reviews may not matter to big-name authors; but they're a tremendous help for first time authors like me, who don't have much following. They will help me to grow my readership by encouraging folks to take a chance on my books.
To put it straight– reviews are the life blood for any author. Please leave your review by clicking below link, it will directly lead you to book review page.
DIRECT REVIEW LINK FOR "Skyrocket Teams to Incredible Heights "

https://www.amazon.com/dp/B09819JJFR

https://www.amazon.in/dp/B09819JJFR

*Y*our support really does make a difference. I'd love to read your review. Thanks again for your support!"

Other Books in Scaling up the Corporate Ladder Series

1.Skyrocket to New Heights

https://www.amazon.com/dp/B08V1BYFQF

Already a best seller in multiple market places and in various categories, it has all ingredients, tips and guidelines to improve one self and skyrocket one's performance to another level. Do buy this book and let me know your feedback

2. Skyrocket Teams to Incredible Heights
https://www.amazon.com/dp/B09819JJFR

3.Skyrocket Leaders to … WIP

https://gitaramachandran.com/

BIBLIOGRAPHY

Pictures for icons are take from Googles Free icon library https://icon-library.com/

<a href="https://icon-library.net/icon/team-icon-vector-7.html">Team Icon Vector #19851</a>

<a href="https://icon-library.net/icon/teams-icon-4.html">Teams Icon #77030</a>

[*1] **Book** 5 Levels of Leadership by John Maxwell

[*2] Management of teams by *Dr. Meredith Belbin.*

- Belbin, R. Meredith (2003), Management teams: why they succeed or fail, 2nd Ed, Butterworth Heinemann, Oxford
- Belbin, R. Meredith (1996), Team roles at Belbin work, Butterworth Heinemann, Oxford

[*3.] Ted Talk by Patrick Lencioni

https://www.ted.com/talks/patrick_lencioni_are_you_an_ideal_team_player?referrer=playlist-how_to_boost_your_team_s_productivity#t-335342

[*4] **Book** : The five dysfunctions of a team by Patrick Lencioni

NB: I have referred to these books and articles for some concepts where I found them to have better authority on that topic before putting my take on Outperforming

Book The Culture Code- The Secrets of Highly Successful Groups by Daniel Coyle

The Big Book of Team Culture

https://activecollab.com/blog/collaboration/how-to-become-a-good-team-leader

Book The Wisdom of Teams: Creating the High-Performance Organization by Jon R. Katzenbach and Douglas K. Smith

Notes from Harvard Mentor

ACKNOWLEDGEMENTS

Mentoring for Writing
and Publishing Book : **Mr Som Batla**

Cover Designed : **Ranjit Jose**
ranjitjos@gmail.com

Editing done by : **Dr. KRS Nair**
keyares51@gmail.com

Community Support : Mr Som Batla's **Author Freedom Hub**

"Throughout this document, 'he' means ' he or she,' and 'his' means 'his/her.'"

COPYRIGHT

Copyright © 2021 by Gita Ramachandran
All rights reserved. No part of this book may be reproduced in any form without permission in writing from the author.
No part of this publication may be reproduced or transmitted in any form or by any means, mechanical or electronic, including photocopying or recording, or by any information storage and retrieval system, or transmitted by email or by any other means whatsoever without permission in writing from the author.